A DRAMATIC DEBUT!

The air was crisp and alive over Jersey City that eighteenth day of April 1946, and in Roosevelt Stadium it fairly crackled with excitement. It was opening day, Montreal against Jersey City. But it was more than that.

Thirty-five thousand fans had jammed the stadium to witness the debut of Jackie Robinson, the first Negro in organized baseball. They had read about his exploits all during the spring training season. They had read of the controversy surrounding his playing in the militantly anti-Negro sections of the South. Now they had come in swarms to see the phenomenon in the flesh, expecting anything to happen, hoping—they didn't quite know for what.

Roosevelt Stadium was like the scene of a giant carnival, or perhaps a great bullfight, or an ancient Roman arena. Only it was Jackie Robinson, instead of the Christians, being thrown to the lions....

JACKIE ROBINSON OF
THE BROOKLYN DODGERS
was originally published
by Julian Messner.

Critics' Corner:

"How Jackie Robinson overcame abuse and paved the way for other members of his race to break into both leagues is dramatically and understandingly told. . . ."
—*Library Journal*

". . . an effectively written and highly dramatic sports biography. . . ."
—*A.L.A. Booklist*

"An excellent contribution. . . . The real heart-warming story in this book is acceptance and the success with which Robinson himself met the challenge."
—*Christian Science Monitor*

Also recommended by: National Council of Teachers of English.

About the Author:

MILTON J. SHAPIRO was born in Brooklyn, New York. While a senior at C.C.N.Y., he got a job as copy boy on a New York newspaper and six months later moved up to the sports department where he covered all the major sports, particularly baseball. He later became sports editor for *The New York Enquirer*. In his spare time he started writing sports biographies, and has become one of the most popular writers in that field.

JACKIE
ROBINSON
of the
BROOKLYN
DODGERS

—————◆—————

Milton J. Shapiro

Illustrated with Photographs

AN ARCHWAY PAPERBACK
POCKET BOOKS • NEW YORK

JACKIE ROBINSON
OF THE BROOKLYN DODGERS

Archway Paperback edition published September, 1967

6th printing.....................August, 1972

L

Published by
POCKET BOOKS, a division of Simon & Schuster, Inc.,
630 Fifth Avenue, New York, N.Y.

Archway Paperback editions are distributed in the U.S.
by Simon & Schuster, Inc., 630 Fifth Avenue, New
York, N.Y. 10020 and in Canada by Simon & Schuster
of Canada, Ltd., Richmond Hill, Ontario, Canada.

To Sharon and Jan,
two young Dodger fans

With grateful acknowledgment to Bill Carr for his help in the preparation of this book

CHAPTER ONE

THE young coach of the Ohio Wesleyan football team lay on his bed in the hotel room at South Bend, Indiana, listening indulgently as the team captain expounded his views on the glories of a career in journalism. "A police reporter, that's the life," the team captain was saying, his eyes shining with the vision of it. He sat on the edge of the bed, idly tossing a football in the air. "Think of it," he exulted, "racing around covering murders and things like that, knowing all the inside stuff going on. That's for me, boy . . ."

A knock on the door cut him short. He frowned, annoyed at the interruption. "Come in," he ordered sharply.

The door swung half open. A maroon-jacketed bellhop poked his head around the edge and surveyed the two men. "One of you guys named Rickey?"

The coach sat up in bed. "That's me," he said.

The bellhop looked at him. "Got a little trouble downstairs. The manager'd like to see you at the desk."

The coach swung his legs off the bed and followed the bellhop down the hall. "Some of the boys cutting up in the lobby?" he asked the boy.

"No, nothing like that."

The two men got into the elevator. "Then what's the trouble?"

The bellhop shifted uncomfortably. "I was just told to get you, that's all. I don't know nothing."

The coach shrugged. Big mystery, he sniffed. He followed the maroon jacket across the lobby to the desk where some of the Wesleyan players were standing, waiting to register.

"What's the trouble?" the coach repeated his question, this time to the hotel manager.

The manager was more forthright than his bellhop. He pointed to a Wesleyan player standing to one side of the desk.

"We don't register niggers in this hotel."

The young coach turned livid. He stared at the hotel manager for a moment, then turned to the player, a tall Negro named Charley Thomas. The big man stood there, his eyes on the floor at his feet, biting his lips savagely to hold back the tears of embarrassment. It was the player's first trip away from home, and the Ohio coach berated himself silently for not warning Thomas of such eventualities. He turned angrily back to the manager. Then, suddenly, his rage subsided.

"Charley," he said softly, without looking at the Negro player, "go sit down for a couple of minutes. We'll see what we can do."

He heard the young man move off, then, checking the edge that threatened to creep into his voice, he spoke to the hotel manager. "Listen," he said earnestly, "I've got plenty of room in my suite. How about putting up a cot there for the fellow?"

The manager shook his head. "Nothing doing. We don't want niggers in this hotel, like I said."

"But look," Branch Rickey said desperately, "we won't register him, just let him stay up there with me. If he can't stay here, we'll have to move the whole team to a different hotel."

This last wasn't true, for Rickey knew that every hotel in South Bend had the same rule, and it would be Thomas, the Negro player, who would have to seek separate accommodations if the hotel remained firm in its position. But Rickey hoped the bluff would work.

He watched the manager's face anxiously as the man thought over his proposition. The coach leaned across the desk. "What do you say—just a cot in the room," he urged.

Finally, the hotel manager shrugged resignedly. "If you want to sleep in the same room with the

3

nigger, it's okay with me, as long as he don't register. But I'll only let it go this one time."

Without a word of thanks Rickey turned and walked over to where Thomas was waiting. "Let's go, Charley," he said. "You're staying with me."

Thomas looked up at him, bewilderment on his face. "But . . ." he whirled to look back at the registration desk. "But the manager said . . ."

"The manager changed his mind," Rickey snapped.

Thomas looked at him searchingly. "Mr. Rickey, I don't want to start any trouble. If you're going to get in any trouble about this I'd just as soon sleep in the park or someplace."

"There's not going to be any trouble," Rickey assured him. "Just grab your things and come on upstairs."

Thomas got up and followed Rickey across the lobby, walking stiffly, conscious of the curious and hostile glances from the loungers in the lobby chairs. In the elevator he pressed into the corner when the operator stared at him, holding the car.

"Up!" Rickey barked. "Up!"

In the suite, Rickey sank wearily into a chair. Thomas sat down carefully on the edge of the bed and looked at his coach.

"Don't let it get you down, Charley," Rickey said quietly. "It's one of the things you're going to run into from time to time. I'm just sorry I didn't warn you about it before we got here."

Thomas nodded. "That's all right, Mr. Rickey. I guess maybe I should have expected it myself."

The two men sat there then, Rickey, slouched in his chair, staring at his shoe tops; Thomas, sitting on the edge of the bed, staring at the wall, his face working, his lips tight. Neither man said a word.

After a while, the tears came to Thomas' eyes. First they welled up until they nearly choked him with the attempt to hold them back, then they overflowed and ran down his face in a torrent of emotion. His body shook uncontrollably as he wept. Suddenly he cried out in anguish and tore at the skin of his hands with his fingernails.

"If only they were white! Oh, God, if only they were white!"

Rickey, shaken, stared at the weeping player. "Charley, what are you doing, Charley!"

The Negro kept clawing at his skin. "It's my hands! My hands! They're black! If only they were white. White! That's all!" His voice broke—and for a moment only the sound of his sobbing filled the room. Then he looked at Rickey, the pain and despair in his eyes.

"I'd be as good as anybody then, wouldn't I, Mr. Rickey, if they were white?" he said.

Rickey bowed his head to hide the mist that clouded his own eyes. "Charley," he said softly, "the day will come when they won't have to be white."

The afternoon sunlight climbed up the walls and turned into the gray light of dusk, and the grayness became the blackness of night. And all that time Branch Rickey remained in his room, slumped in his chair, listening to the other man cry. He let the sound of it burn into his memory, and the sight of the young Negro tearing at the flesh of his hands etched itself forever in his eyes. And he knew these harrowing hours would haunt him always.

So it was, in the year 1910, that the seed was sown. And it would lie dormant in the mind of Branch Rickey for nearly two generations, to be nurtured and germinated by events, waiting for the moment when the climate would be ready for its blossoms. And that time would come at last in 1945, and two years later would bear fruit. Sweet fruit to some, bitter to others.

This is the Jackie Robinson story. And that's how it really began.

CHAPTER TWO

THE porch was shady and cool in the heat of the Georgia afternoon, and Mallie Robinson sat there on the creaking rocker, letting the light breeze from the creek dry the perspiration off her glistening face. She looked out over the vastness of the plantation, squinting into the brightness of the May sun. In a way, she thought, she would regret leaving. A body could get along tolerably well in Cairo, she had always said, long as he minded his own business. But she just couldn't work the land any more. Not with Jerry gone.

She let her mind dwell on her husband for a moment. Maybe you couldn't blame Jerry too much, she thought tolerantly. Running away like that. With five kids coming pretty quick, and only half-cropping the land, by the time they got through paying half of what they raised to the man who owned the plantation, there wasn't much left. Enough maybe to keep the Robinsons in greens and side meat, but sometimes a man needs more than that to want to keep going.

Mallie Robinson sighed. Anyway, Jerry Robinson up and took off. Went to Florida, she heard. Now here she was on the land with five little ones —and the oldest just ten. She had taken the horse and hitched up the plow and tried. The straps of the plow harness had bit deep into her shoulders and left them red and raw, but she turned the earth from the first light of morning until the relentless heat of the afternoon ran the sweat into her eyes and soaked her body through the thin cotton wrapper. Then the wetness would make the harness straps bite deeper, chafing the rawness of her bruised flesh, and she would cry out in despair and flee to the dark coolness of the porch on the front of the gray clapboard shack. And she would read the letter.

She took the letter from her pocket, as she sat there on the rocker. She had read it a dozen times since its arrival the week before. It was damp now and some of the writing was smeared. But she knew the words practically without reading them. Unfolding the letter on her lap and smoothing out the pages with her hand, she read again the words of her brother Burton, about how good things were out in California. The weather was fine, warm and sunny, but never so brutally hot like Cario could get. You could raise a good crop, especially in the valleys, or, if Mallie wanted, she could get a job in the city and move in with Burton for a while. And Burton would send her a little money so she could take a bus and come out there with the kids.

It had been nearly three years since Mallie had seen her brother. Burton was a cook, and when the doctor he'd been cooking for in Georgia had gone into the Army for the war, he'd taken Burton along with him. They were stationed in California for a while, and Burton liked it so much that he went back there to live when the war was over.

Now it was 1920, and it was getting time for Mallie Robinson to make up her mind. She held the letter in her hands and looked out at the untended land. Suddenly a child's sharp cry came from inside the house. Mallie stuffed the letter back into her pocket and hurried wearily inside. She walked swiftly into the small, gloomily dark bedroom and looked down at the wailing infant in the rickety wooden crib.

"John Roosevelt Robinson," she scolded. "You are the cryin'est child I ever did see." She picked up her sixteen-month-old youngest born and cradled him in her arms. "Now you better learn to hush," she admonished, "or we're goin' to leave you behind when we go to Uncle Burton in California."

Mallie had made up her mind. The next day she

told the plantation owner she was leaving, and she wrote to Burton to send whatever he could spare; she would sell her few possessions to get up the rest of the fare.

So on a May morning the Robinsons boarded a bus with just the clothing on their backs and a few personal belongings in a pair of aged suitcases stored in the luggage compartment. Mallie had packed a small overnight bag with sandwiches of cold meat and cheese; the bus would stop at many places, she knew, which would not serve Negroes. She picked out seats in the back of the bus for her family. Edgar, ten years old, Frank, eight, and Matthew, six, she sat together. With her she kept Willa Mae, four, and little Jackie, sixteen months.

The bus roared off, winding through the streets of Cairo, and then turned onto the big highway and headed west. All day and night they rode, then the Robinsons got off and were shifted to another bus. And the nights turned into days and back into nights again, with the Robinsons constantly changing busses. The children became hungry and restless, but Mallie shushed them and threatened them into silence. Finally one morning, after riding for a long time in the mountains, they came out on a wide green plain. And before the day was over they were in Pasadena.

Mallie wasted no time feeling sorry for herself. The night she arrived she bedded the children in

Burton's house and then sat down and had a long talk with her brother.

"You goin' to find a job for me tomorrow, Burton?" she asked right out.

"Now hold on there a minute, Mallie," her brother grinned at her. "Why don't you kind of take things a little easy for a couple of days? Get settled down here with the kids. See about gettin' 'em in school. You can find a job next week as good as tomorrow."

"I didn't come all the way out here to sit around and eat off your table. I want to work—and I want to find my own place to live."

"Who's goin' to watch out for the kids, Mallie?"

"The kids'll watch out for each other. They did in Cairo. They can do it here."

Burton shook his head. "It ain't goin' to be easy for you, Mallie."

"You think it's been easy even one day since Jerry's gone?" she snorted. "I ain't lookin' for easy. I'm lookin' to live, and help my kids live better than you and me did, Burton."

"I got no complaints, Mallie."

His sister leaned forward across the kitchen table. "Listen, Burton. Our pap was a slave. We done better. You better'n me. But we neither of us done very much. I'd like to see my boys come up more than a cook in a white man's kitchen. Like for Willa Mae to do more than scrub a floor, break her back doin' somebody else's washin'. Can they do it here, Burton? Can colored folks do better'n that in California, Burton?"

Mallie Robinson soon found her own answer. With her brother's help, she arranged to take in washing and ironing. As quickly as she could she rented an apartment of her own, but before long she was back with Burton again to cut down her expenses.

"It won't be for long, Burton," she promised her brother. "I got an idea in my head. If I can save a little money, I'm gonna buy a house of my own and rent out rooms."

Out Mallie went to drum up more washing and ironing. Usually she had to work in people's homes, and the Robinson children took care of themselves, went to school and found odd jobs afterward to help out at home. Jackie, the youngest, not yet of school age, was a problem for a while.

"Willa Mae," Mallie Robinson said to her daughter one day, "you take your little brother to school with you from now on."

Willa Mae looked bewildered. "I can't take Jackie with me, Ma," she said. "He's only four. They won't let him in."

Her mother nodded. "He don't have to go to the class. You just sit him out there in the yard to play when you go in every morning, and you take him home with you when you get out. That

12

way he won't get in mischief, and I'll know where he is."

Off Jackie went the next morning. All day he sat in the sand piles by himself or played on the slides. Occasionally Willa Mae was able to steal a glance out the window to see that he was all right.

By the time Jackie was in school learning his ABC's, he had already learned to make money. His first job was watering the flowers for an uncle who lived near by. Then he hauled his little red wagon around town, gathering newspapers and odd bits of trash and selling them to a junkman.

He picked up arithmetic the hard way, making change on his shoeshine route along the streets of Pasadena. He sold hot dogs at the Rose Bowl, caddied at the local golf courses, and every Sunday morning he got up at four o'clock and delivered newspapers.

The money Jackie and his brothers picked up began to mean more than pocket money to the family. Their mother had bought that house she wanted, and rented out the spare rooms. But then came 1929 and 1930, the bad years. The roomers couldn't pay the rent, but Mallie didn't have the heart to send them into the street. There was less and less washing and ironing to take in—people had to do their own those days.

The Robinsons still had the roof over their heads, but food was becoming a problem. They were down to eating one meal a day. Then some days there were no meals, unless one of the teachers at school provided the children with milk and a sandwich.

The Robinsons were poor; yet somehow they were happy. Every Sunday morning they marched to the Negro Methodist church in their neighborhood, and Mallie Robinson gave thanks for being guided to California.

"We're hungry," Mallie would say to herself in the cool silence of the church, "but so are all our neighbors. And the boys and Willa Mae are doin' fine in school. Good schools. White folks schools. They're gonna be all right. And when the Lord wills it that folks should be working and eating regular again, we're gonna be, too. A body can't ask for anything fairer than that. And that's all Mallie Robinson is asking for, Lord. What's right and fair for her kids."

CHAPTER THREE

It is practically impossible to pinpoint the exact moment racial prejudice first hits home to a child; when he realizes for the first time that the color of his skin differs from that of most of the other children in the neighborhood; when he realizes that this difference makes him a special target for taunts, insults, slurs, physical attacks, deprivation of opportunity, a hundred different manifestations of the psychological distillate of man's fears and anxieties.

But the day inevitably comes when a Negro suddenly knows he is a Negro. What he feels, with this realization, is difficult even for a Negro to assay.

Was there a hurt or mere puzzlement? Did he feel a self-defensive, retaliatory hate? Was there bitterness, resentment, anger? Was he overcome by despair—or fired by determination?

He is always asked, if he is ever asked at all,

many years afterward, and time and memory blunt the sensations, as they blur the moment.

The moment for Jackie Robinson might well have been a spring morning when he was about ten years old.

It was one of Jackie's chores each morning before school to sweep the sidewalk in front of his house. That painfully memorable morning a little white girl, about Jackie's own age, emerged from her house directly across the street and began sweeping her sidewalk, too.

The girl looked over at Jackie. "You got the dirtiest sidewalk on the whole block," she taunted with the innocent teasing of her years.

Jackie took the bait. "I have not," he called back. "You've got the dirtiest sidewalk. And the dirtiest house, too," he retorted.

The little girl stamped her foot. "And you've got the dirtiest old house in Pasadena, I'll bet!" she shouted.

"You're just a girl. What do you know?"

"I know more than you any old day!"

"Yeah, go on and sweep your dirty sidewalk!"

"Go on and sweep yourself, you dirty nigger!"

Jackie stared at her, then stooped quickly, picked up a stone and hurled it across the street. The girl picked up a stone and threw back. Jackie threw another one, and back and forth the missiles were hurled. Neither child was getting hit, but then the girl started screaming.

"Mommy! Daddy! Mommy! Daddy!"

The girl's father charged out the front door. He took the situation in with a glance. "Get out of here, you little nigger!" he bawled at Jackie. "Get out of here before I break your neck!"

"I live here," Jackie shouted back defiantly. "Anyway, she started it."

"Yeah, well I'll finish it! I'll teach you, you dirty little nigger!"

The man picked up a handful of stones and began throwing them at Jackie, who took refuge behind a tree and threw back. And the two stood there, the man and the ten-year-old boy, shouting at each other and hurling stones back and forth across the street.

Jackie's mother tried to come out to stop the fight, but as she inched open the front door a barrage of stones from across the street sent her into the house for safety.

Finally, the man's wife came to the front door. A barrage of missiles met her, too, and she retreated. But from inside the doorway she began calling to her husband.

"Stop that stupid stone throwing! Aren't you ashamed, fighting like that with a little boy!"

But the war went on, unabated. Meanwhile,

Jackie's brothers, Frank, Edgar, and Mack, slipped out the front door in the face of the man's fire and joined Jackie in the fight. They kept out of the throwing, but raced around gathering ammunition for their younger brother.

Finally, the man's wife braved the flying stones and ran out of the house. She grabbed her husband by the arm and dragged him, protesting, back into the house, followed by the jeers of the Robinson brothers.

The victory was Jackie's, but things could never be the same for him. Although he was involved in few racial incidents in those years, if he didn't realize it before, he was aware of it now—his skin was black. Whatever he did or said would almost always be received and judged by white people with that qualification in mind.

The Robinsons were the only Negro family on their block, but there was no animosity shown toward them, before or after the rock-throwing incident. Jackie and his brothers went to school and played with white boys, Japanese, Mexicans and other Negroes.

Still, his best friends were Roscoe Devore and Ernie Cunningham, both Negroes.

He was bright and quick in his early school years. His proficiency at games even then was winning him popularity with his friends and schoolmates. It stood him in good stead during the hungry Depression years.

"Hey, Jackie," one of his better-off classmates would say. "I'll give you an apple if you'll be on my team."

Jackie accepted the bribes gladly. His growling stomach took sides with the highest bidder for his services, and often he would accumulate enough fruit, cookies and candy to take home for a feast with his brothers and sister.

He was not the only trophy gatherer in the family, however. Mack was beginning to make a name for himself in the sports world. Always a fast runner, in high school he starred on the track team, despite several doctors' warnings that something was wrong with his heart.

At Pasadena Junior College and the University of Oregon he was practically a one-man track team, setting coast records that stand today. The doctors continued to warn him about his heart, but Mack persisted.

"I'm going to run if it kills me," he said.

Jackie idolized his big brother. When Mack went to the 1936 Olympics in Berlin, the Robinsons sat by the radio to hear the account of the race. "I'm going to be like Mack when I grow up," Jackie said, his face glowing with pride.

But Mrs. Robinson hardly heard him. She was worried about Mack and his heart. Worried that the

19

strain of the competition might overcome his will and courage.

They were broadcasting the two-hundred-meter sprint now. As the announcer followed the runners, no mention was made of Mack.

"Hey, where's Mack?" Jackie wondered aloud.

His mother remained silent, white lipped with fear that her son had been stricken in one of the earlier events.

Then came the announcement of the finish.

"The winner, for the United States, Jesse Owens. In second place, for the United States, Matthew Robinson . . ."

Jackie leaped in the air. "Second place! Right behind Jesse Owens!"

Mallie Robinson prayed her thanks silently.

Soon she had another son to worry about with his sports playing. Jackie began to develop a taste for sand-lot football. He didn't weigh very much, but he liked the competitive spirit of the game. He was fast, aggressive, unafraid, and in the games on the corner lots he invariably played in the backfield.

Carrying the ball was Jackie's greatest love then. Time after time he would charge into the ragged line of youngsters, disappearing finally in a tangle of arms and legs. But not before he gained yardage, and added a few more bruises to his battered body. Hardly any of the youngsters could afford the simplest protective equipment, but they played football as hard as any helmeted, shoulder- and hip-padded teams. It was a tribute to their gameness and toughness that few of them ever came out of a game because of injuries.

Often Jackie would come home with the scars of battle on his face and body—scrapes, purple bruises, scratches, lumps. His mother would shake her head in despair.

"Jackie, someday they're going to carry you home with a broken leg or something. Can't you play anything else but football?"

And he would grin at her from swollen lips. "Sure I can, Mom. Only this happens to be the football season."

When the baseball season came around, Jackie played, but rather indifferently. Although he was good at the game, baseball somehow didn't give him the "kick" football did. Perhaps it was because there was no Negro star in the baseball world with whom to identify himself, the way youngsters are prone to do when they're sports minded.

However, there were Negro stars in the Pacific Coast professional football league, and it was likely that this factor, plus the more natural outlet football provided for his aggressiveness and competitive spirit, that shaped his preference for the gridiron sport.

When he entered Muir Technical High School,

Jackie went out for every sport. He starred in football, basketball, track and baseball. In his senior year, the local papers began talking about "one of Muir Tech's all-time great athletes, an all-around performer named Jackie Robinson."

The worst years of the Depression were over by the time Jackie was ready to think about college. Still, the Robinsons were far from well off. To Mallie Robinson there was no problem.

"What college you figure on going to, Jackie?" she queried her youngest son in his senior year at Muir.

Jackie had his mind pretty well made up. And he knew his mother had, too. Yet . . .

"Mom, you honestly think we can afford to let me go?"

"Let's not hear any more of that now," she glared. "You think I'm going to let you pass a chance to go to college? Don't you know what it means that you can even talk about *maybe* going, if you want to? Don't you know what that means?"

"Sure I do, but . . ."

"Never you mind, but! You get yourself some kind of part-time job while you go to college, to help out yourself and your ma. But you go. You hear me, John Roosevelt Robinson?"

Jackie grinned and put his arms around his mother's shoulders.

"You're a great woman, Mom. I won't let you down."

"Not me, Jackie. Whatever you do, son, you won't be letting me down." Mallie Robinson shook her head soberly.

"Don't let yourself down, Jackie. Or your race."

CHAPTER FOUR

Wearing the basketball uniform of Pasadena Junior College, Jackie Robinson dribbled into forecourt and looked for a teammate to pass off to. He tried to shake off the tide of anger that was rising in him. That's what he wants, Jackie thought. He's trying to make me start a fight. Well . . . He stopped and dribbled the ball in place, looking around. Dimly in the background he heard the noise of the crowd, the calls of his teammates. His eye caught the player on the enemy team, the white player who had been taunting him ever since the game began. The fellow was grinning at him now, sneering at him, challenging him with his obvious prejudice.

Jackie moved in, then passed the ball across court. He cut in and behind his guard quickly, took a return pass, dove in toward the basket, leaped for a toss at the hoop. As he went up he felt a player leap up with him; as he threw the ball he felt an elbow jam roughly into his ribs. The blow threw off his aim; the ball hit the rim and bounced off, the rebound going to the enemy. Jackie dashed back toward his own basket. Running at his side was the player who had given him the elbow. It was the player who had been goading him all night. Jackie wasn't surprised.

The player grinned at him now, as they raced together downcourt. "Too bad, nigger," he said.

Jackie gritted his teeth, but he made no reply. His answer was to pick off an enemy pass and return to the attack, leading his teammates as he had been all night, all season.

Pasadena opened up a commanding lead, Jackie continuing his playmaking and scoring. As the margin between the two teams widened, his tormentor increased the frequency and viciousness of his racial attacks.

In a scramble under Pasadena's basket he tripped Jackie, sending him crashing to the hardwood floor. The referee's whistle shrilled the foul. Jackie rose slowly to his feet. The enemy player hovered menacingly above him, hands on hips. Jackie stood face to face with the other player. The anger was boiling in him now. His eyes blazed.

"Why don't you stick to playing basketball, fellow?" he said quietly.

"Why don't you shut your black face?" came the

retort. "If you don't like the way I play, start something!"

Jackie clenched his fists. He was quivering with his effort at restraint. He started to say something, checked himself and started to turn away.

"Niggers never did have any guts!" came the challenge.

Jackie whirled. "Okay. If that's the way you want it. Meet me outside after the game."

"What's the matter with right now?" the other shot back.

He leaped at Jackie, who retreated, blocking the blows. With a flash of instinct he knew the consequences of fighting back against a white player on the court. Quickly the players and referees separated the two men. The deliberate fouling of Jackie had not gone unnoticed by the referees, and they sent him to the foul line to take his free throw. Then they turned to the other player. "You're out of the game, mister. You ought to be ashamed of yourself."

Pasadena went on to win the game, led by Jackie, as it had been all season. Coach Carl Metton that year had a great team at Pasadena, with Robinson and teammate Bill Busick, who later starred at Annapolis, among the leading scorers in the Pacific Coast Junior College Division.

There was no off season in sports for Jackie at Pasadena. When the basketball season ended, the baseball and track and field season began. Events for the two sports occasionally took place on the same day, but it was nothing for Jackie to compete in track in the morning, then take off for the baseball diamond in the afternoon.

On one such busy morning, Jackie set a new junior college broad jump mark, with a leap of twenty-five feet, six and one-third inches, a feat not often equaled today in college competition.

But as Jackie walked off the field that morning, he accepted the congratulations of his coach and teammates glumly.

"I feel kind of bad," he remarked to a friend, "setting that record."

"Bad!" came the retort. "What for?"

"The old twenty-five-foot record was held by my brother Mack, that's why."

In September, 1939, Jackie Robinson entered the University of California at Los Angeles. The coaches of the UCLA teams awaited him eagerly, particularly Babe Horrell, the football coach.

The UCLA Bruins were a T-formation team, a system based on speed and deception. Horrell knew that Jackie would fit into the attack perfectly, and would especially complement the threat of another talented Negro football player on that squad, Kenny Washington. Robinson was fast, daring, tricky, a man difficult to bring down once he got through the line into the secondary; Washington was a hard-charging powerhouse who bulled his way through the line, tearing open holes with his high knee-action rushes.

Jackie's running made itself felt in the opening game of the season. It was the fourth quarter of a 7-7 tie with the University of Washington. Playing safety man for UCLA on defense—the Bruins didn't have offense-defense platoons in those days —Jackie caught a Washington punt on his own thirty-yard line, and took off.

He ran right through the entire Huskie team, zigzagging and swivel-hipping his way down the field, until he was finally dragged down on the Washington five-yard line, a run of sixty-five yards.

Kenny Washington bulled over for the score, and UCLA won the game, 14–7.

The next game was against Stanford. In the fourth quarter the Indians were leading 14–7, led by the passing of the great Frankie Albert. Now they were on the march again, moving into UCLA territory. Again and again Albert's passes found their mark. The clock was ticking away.

Robinson had been watching Albert's tactics carefully, thought he noticed a pattern to the plays that were being called. As the next play unfolded, he tracked a Stanford end toward the sideline, and was rewarded as Albert threw a pass to Jackie's man.

Robinson leaped into the air and picked off the

pass deep in his own territory. He shook off one Stanford tackler, another, then he swiveled free and streaked for the Stanford goal. He was brought down on the Indians' eight-yard line.

Two plays later, UCLA scored, to make the score 14–13. Then Jackie calmly kicked the extra point to tie the game, just before the final gun sounded.

UCLA rolled through Montana, Oregon, Washington State and California. Kenny Washington was getting most of the headlines, but Jackie Robinson was right behind him. And just how valuable he was to the UCLA team was proved right before the game with Santa Clara.

In a practice scrimmage, Jackie tried to twist away from a tackler and sprained his left ankle. He played out the last three games of the season, but the injury slowed him considerably. It slowed, too, the entire Bruin offense. UCLA had to be content with tying the remaining three games.

Jackie's record that season was one of the best on the coast, though his injury hobbled him for the three final games. He scored twenty-six points on four touchdowns and two extra points. He was third on the coast in individual offense, with a total of five hundred and nineteen yards rushing, and a sensational average of over twelve yards gained every time he carried the ball.

Despite the continuing soreness of his ankle,

Jackie moved right into the basketball season and was a sensation. Playing against the greatly favored California team, he kept UCLA in the game all the way with amazing floor work and accurate shooting. With seconds to go, and the score tied, Jackie intercepted a California pass, drove down the length of the court and tossed in a basket that gave UCLA a stunning 35–33 upset victory.

In basketball there was no Kenny Washington to take the headlines. The newspaper sport sections were full of Jackie Robinson's exploits on the basketball court. Opponents tried screening him out, double-teaming him, fouling him, riding him—everything.

He was a demon on the floor, a beautiful playmaker with perfect timing and amazing deception. He was one of the best shots in college basketball. And through it all, he was always a team man.

Toward the end of the season he was in a scoring race with Ralph Vaughn of Southern California. Yet playing against Stanford in a close game, he repeatedly fed his teammates while Stanford double-teamed him, and froze the ball to protect UCLA's slim lead in the closing minutes. Despite this, he scored twenty-three points in the game.

When the season ended, Jackie was leading scorer of the Pacific Coast Conference—Southern Division, with one hundred and forty-eight points, an average of more than twelve a game.

Came spring—and the track and field and baseball seasons. In the former sport, he won the Pacific Coast Conference title in the broad jump.
He was hoping to make the United States Olympic
team, following in the footsteps of his brother
Mack, but the outbreak of war in Europe canceled
all thought of holding the Olympic games.

Baseball was more a lark than a sport for Jackie.
He was easily good enough to make shortstop on
the team, and in one game stole five bases, including
home twice. But he was only a fair hitter and less
than a fair fielder in 1940.

Kenny Washington was gone when the 1940 football season opened, and the Bruin eleven wasn't
much that year. Jackie was a one-man team, the
only thing that gave UCLA partisans reason to
cheer as the Bruins lost game after game.

He ran eighty-seven yards to score the only goal
in the loss to Southern Methodist. He held one of
the greatest Stanford teams of all time to a
20–14 margin, then scored two touchdowns and
passed for another in UCLA's only win of the
season, over Washington State.

Things weren't going so well at home that year,
either. His mother was working, but her brother
Burton was getting old and was ailing. Edgar was
married and raising a family, so was Willa Mae.
Mack had had to quit Oregon to come home and
work.

31

Jackie was beginning to feel guilty about remaining in college under these conditions. UCLA was a tuition-free school, but there were plenty of incidental expenses. He took on jobs selling candy and hot dogs at the Rose Bowl games, worked as a bus boy in a cafeteria and was a part-time janitor at the college.

Then Mack got married. The money situation was getting tighter and tighter. Jackie was growing more restless each day. Despite his college training, Mack wasn't making out too well.

What's the use of it all? Jackie began to think. What will I do when I finish college? Maybe I ought to quit now, get out and work, help things at home.

He began to scout the job situation. The government needed leaders for its National Youth Administration program, men who could qualify as physical education instructors, who could supervise games, sports, calisthenics.

Jackie made up his mind.

It was the spring of 1941. The basketball season was over. Again Jackie had been high scorer for his section of the Pacific Coast Conference. He had also become the first four-letter man in the history of UCLA.

But that was behind him now. During dinner one spring evening he made known his plans to quit college.

"I've been thinking about it for quite a while, Mom," he said. "I'm sure it's the best thing for me to do."

His mother didn't take it quietly, "What do you mean, you're going to quit school?" she demanded. "You're so close to graduating, to getting a degree, and now you're going to quit? It don't make sense. It's just like you're throwing away all the years you been in school. You might as well have quit when you were in high school as quit now. Without a degree, you're nothing, Jackie!"

Mack, who was there for dinner that night, agreed.

"Look at me, Jackie. I quit—and I'm not setting any worlds on fire, you know. Okay, I had to quit to go to work, and I'm not crying about it. But you can hold out a little more, can't you, get a good job somewhere?"

But Jackie wouldn't budge. "It just doesn't pay," he said firmly. "Maybe I'll be sorry later, but right now I feel I can do just about as well without a degree. And brother, don't try to tell me a few extra dollars a week won't be welcome around this house."

They continued their arguments in vain.

"I can get along fine without your money," Mallie contended. "I got along when all of you were too little to wipe your own noses, and I can still do it."

Jackie hesitated a moment. "Look, Mom, Mack. It isn't only money for the house and myself I'm thinking about. I'm thinking about the future."

Mack looked at him inquiringly. "What do you mean, future?"

Jackie appeared embarrassed. He shifted in his chair.

"Well, you know . . . I mean Rachel."

Mack chuckled, and for the first time since the discussion began, Mallie Robinson smiled.

Rachel. So that was it. She understood now. It wasn't so bad, if it was Rachel.

"She's a good girl, Rachel," Mallie Robinson said to her son.

"The best, Mom," Jackie said soberly.

"You tell her yet? About your quitting?"

Jackie shook his head.

Mallie smiled knowingly. "If I know Rachel Isum, she's not going to let you off easy."

CHAPTER FIVE

SHE was tall and slim and pretty. Jackie had noticed her at once when she walked into the student lounge at UCLA with another girl and Ray Bartlett, his best friend at school. Ray brought the girls over to where Jackie was standing, broom in hand, sweeping the lounge as part of his janitor's duties.

"Rachel Isum, Jackie Robinson," Ray made the introductions. Jackie already knew the other girl.

"Hello, Rachel."

"Hello, Jackie. My friends call me Rae."

He nodded. He was feeling awkward, unsure of himself. Girls were things he'd never had much time for.

Bartlett waited for Jackie to say something. But he saw his friend as usual was tongue-tied in the presence of girls.

He shrugged. "Say, Jackie," he took the initiative himself, "there's that football dance coming up Saturday night, isn't there?"

Jackie nodded. He was looking at Rachel. Her eyes were smiling at him.

Bartlett realized now he'd have to do this himself. Jackie was too smitten to say a word.

"So about this dance," Bartlett continued. "Hey, are you listening to me, Jackie?"

Robinson forced his attention away from the girl. He looked at Bartlett. "Yeah, sure, Ray, you were talking about a dance."

Bartlett grinned. "Well, good for you. I thought you had left us for a while. Listen, about the dance, how about making a double date out of it? Me and my girl and you and Rachel."

Robinson appeared embarrassed. He avoided looking at Rachel. "Well, I don't know, Ray. Aren't you kind of putting Rachel on the spot, asking like this? Maybe she doesn't want to go. She just met me, you know."

Rachel laughed. Jackie looked at her. Her eyes were dancing, teasing him. "Who's got who on a spot, Mr. Robinson?" She turned to Bartlett. "Maybe your friend doesn't want to take me to the dance, Ray."

"Oh, no," Jackie said quickly. "I mean, I'd be happy to. I'd like to. Only I . . . I don't know. I don't want you to go because Ray is asking you in front of me. You know what I mean?"

She laughed again. That laugh got to Jackie. It was warm. She put her hand on his arm. "Don't worry about me, Jackie. I'm not that polite. If I didn't want to go with you, I'd have kicked Ray in the shins so hard they'd have heard him yelling all over Kerckhoff Hall."

Jackie and Rachel saw a lot of each other after that. She was good for him, he knew that. His aggressiveness in sports was accompanied by a quick temper and mercurial moodiness. He never threw his weight around unnecessarily on the gridiron or basketball court, but he never backed away, either.

Negroes in college sports were no novelty on the West Coast, and overt incidents on the playing field were avoided. But there was a point beyond which most Negro athletes hesitated to venture. Arguing openly with a white player was one of them.

But not for Jackie. On the field he fought loudly and long when he thought he was right, and it never occurred to him to back off because the other player was white.

Rachel helped to calm him down. During those days at UCLA, she told him what she was to tell him again and again during the course of his exciting career in baseball.

"Jackie," she chided softly, "your temper is your worst enemy."

He found that he could talk himself out to her. When rage tore at him, when frustration gnawed at his insides, he sought her company and poured loose his emotions as he never could before.

This was particularly so in his second year at UCLA, when the basketball and football teams were taking defeat after defeat. Jackie and Rachel would be sitting at a booth in a luncheonette near the campus, and he would replay each game, angry at himself and his teammates for not playing better, for missing opportunities.

"If only . . ." he would begin, and Rachel would interrupt him.

"Jackie, how many times have I told you it does no good to tear at yourself this way? You can't relive every game, every play. What's done is done. All this isn't going to score any touchdowns, or put a ball through the basket. You play the best you can—and forget about it."

It helped. Rachel couldn't cure his hotheadedness, his depressions, his bitterness. They were imbedded too deeply in Jackie's personality, rooted by the experiences of his years. But she softened them with her wisdom and her patience.

Now he was on his way to meet her, to tell her that the dreams they dreamed together had been lost to unyielding reality. A degree for Jackie, a career, a future, these would have to give way to the necessity for money right now.

38

Rachel wouldn't like it. She would argue, eloquently, as she often did. But this time, he knew, there would be no arguments she could muster to dissuade him.

He took a deep breath and pushed open the door of the luncheonette.

Rachel was sitting at their favorite booth, in the back, near the jukebox. Jackie slid in opposite her and ordered two coffees. She waited till the waiter brought their cups and left, then she spoke for the first time.

"You sounded funny when you called and asked me to meet you here, Jackie. Something the matter?"

He didn't look at her. He stirred his coffee absently, staring into the steaming liquid as though for an answer. Then he raised his head and looked at Rachel.

"I'm quitting school. I'm taking a job as assistant athletic director with the National Youth Administration."

She tried to keep the shock from her voice. "But Jackie—" she began, but he held up his hand.

"No," he said. "Let me tell it first. Tell it all. Then you can talk."

It poured out of him then. The words tumbled from his lips, edged sometimes with bitterness, sometimes with anger, sometimes with pleading despair. He told her all, the hopes and the years of

no hope, the victories and the defeats, the accep-
tances and the rejections.

And there was Mom and Mack and Willa Mae
and old Uncle Burton. And money.

When he was finished he looked into her face
and waited. She didn't speak.

"Well," Jackie offered. "Now tell me I'm crazy
as usual."

Rachel shook her head.

Jackie pursed his lips. "No arguments? No lectures?"

She smiled at him softly. "No arguments. No
lectures."

Rachel reached across the table and took his
hands in her own. She knew there was a time to
argue with a man, and a time to stand behind him,
no matter what. She knew Jackie, knew the turmoil
he must be feeling, knew how he must have racked
and tortured himself before coming to this decision. No, this was not the time for arguments.
Instead, she sat with him in the luncheonette booth
and held his hands for a long time.

After a while, he dared to look into her eyes.

"Your coffee's getting cold," he said.

"Hm-hmm."

"Another cup?"

"Uh-uh." Her eyes were smiling again.

He had to grin at her. "I guess I shut you up
good."

"What kind of job is this thing, Jackie?" she asked.

"It's a government job, Rachel. Up at Atascadero, north of L.A. Working with kids at the work camp the government's got set up there. Kids living the way I did when I was their age. I think maybe I can do some good."

She nodded. "Yes, you probably can."

"It doesn't pay a heck of a lot, but I won't be needing much for myself up there. I'll be able to send some home to Mom for herself and Uncle Burton, and put aside a little bit for me, for . . . well, you know, maybe someday . . ." He shrugged.

She tried not to smile at his shyness. "Someday?" she asked, teasing him with a straight face.

"Well, uh . . . you know . . ." Then he saw her eyes were laughing and he grinned embarrassedly. "Ah, come on, Rachel!"

She laughed aloud then and touched his hands again.

"Oh, Jackie," she said. Then, "Let's have that fresh cup of coffee now, okay?"

CHAPTER SIX

THE letter came one morning in April of 1942. Jackie Robinson was expecting it. He didn't bother to open it at first. He knew what the letter would say. He sat for a while staring at the envelope, then finally tore it open and began to read.

Thousands of other young men in the United States at that approximate moment were opening the same kind of letter, and, as many of them did, Jackie smiled at the salutation.

"Greetings . . ." the letter began.

Jackie sighed. He softly hummed aloud the opening bars, "You're in the Army Now." Then he grinned. So much for planning and figuring your life, he thought. Who was it, Robert Burns? He tried to recall his college English courses. Burns, was it, who said, "The best laid schemes o' mice and men gang aft a-gley"?

He smiled mentally. A lot of water had gone

under the bridge since he decided to quit UCLA more than a year ago.

The work camp had closed down after several months, leaving him without a job. Then he was asked to play with the college All-Stars against the professional Chicago Bears in the annual Chicago *Tribune* charity game in that city. Jackie looked good enough, playing in a losing cause, to receive an offer from the Los Angeles Bulldogs.

The Bulldogs had several games booked on a barnstorming tour in Hawaii. Would Jackie join them? The money was good; Jackie joined them.

While in Hawaii, Jackie received another offer, this one to play on the college All-Star basketball squad when he got back to the States.

He began to think. Maybe this is where I belong. In sports. The money's pretty good, I like the life. And they seem to want me. Pro basketball, maybe that's it. I can play for plenty of years, make good money, then maybe coach or something, or go into some kind of business.

Well, first things first, he decided. When I get back to the States, I'll have to scout up a job with the pros.

That was in November, 1941. Six short months ago. What did all his thinking mean now? What did anything mean now? He thought of Rachel. He looked down at the letter. "Greetings . . ." He laughed to himself.

After a short while at the reception center in California, Jackie was shipped to a cavalry outfit stationed at Fort Riley, Kansas. It was still the original horse cavalry then, and during his thirteen weeks of basic training he learned plenty about horses.

However, he also learned that the Army was looking for Negro officers. He applied at once for officers' training school, was admitted, and graduated as second lieutenant early in 1943.

His basic training had been cavalry, so it was only natural that the Army assign him as an officer back into the cavalry. Only this time it was with the newly formed armored cavalry—the 761st Tank Battalion of the Second Armored Division being trained at Camp Hood, Texas.

A tank platoon was assigned to Jackie's command, and he leaned to his task with eagerness. But the rigors of the tank corps training aggravated an old football injury. Bone chips in his ankle began to move and inflamed the joint. He tried to ignore the pain at first, then the swelling became so pronounced it was impossible for him to pull on his boots. Regretfully, Jackie turned himself into the base hospital. By the time he got out, his unit had been shipped overseas. He was placed on limited service and spent the rest of his time in the Army touring camps as a morale and recreation officer.

In December of 1944 Jackie was given his honorable discharge. But not before he'd had a very important conversation with a Negro soldier he'd met in one army camp.

It was while he was acting as recreation officer, organizing sports activities. One of the Negro GI's at the camp suggested to Jackie that they organize several baseball teams from the various units.

"I used to play with the Kansas City Monarchs," the fellow said. "I can help out and sort of look after things when you move on."

Jackie agreed it was a good idea.

After several games had been played, in which Jackie had participated, the GI came forward again.

"Say, Lieutenant, you play a mighty fine game of shortstop out there," he said.

Jackie grinned. "Oh, I dabble a little."

The GI grinned back. "You ever think of playing pro ball?"

Robinson looked at him inquiringly. "Pro ball?"

"Yes, sir. You know, the Negro leagues."

Jackie shook his head. "Never thought about it. Doesn't sound very tempting."

"Oh, it's not bad, Lieutenant. Not bad at all. Of course you got to travel around a lot, and you play lots of ball, two games a day maybe three, four days in a row sometimes. But it's better than digging ditches, and it pays a lot more, too."

Jackie shrugged absently. "I don't know. Maybe I'll give it a thought. Thanks, anyway."

The other man nodded. "When you get out, just get in touch with the Monarchs any time you feel like playing. Tell them I told you to. They're always looking for good players."

Jackie recalled this conversation several months after he'd been separated from service. He was then in Austin, Texas, as athletic director of the all-Negro Sam Houston College.

It was an economically poor college; the pay was small. And the old money question had come again to Jackie's mind.

There was Rachel, waiting patiently for him in California, waiting for the time he could honestly say they were financially free to carry out their plans. And there was Mom—and Uncle Burton who was now bedridden.

How could he ever make enough money for everything, buried in the struggling economic morass of a Negro college?

So Jackie Robinson's thoughts turned to his conversation with the GI about the Kansas City Monarchs. And that evening he wrote a letter to Houston, Texas, where the Monarchs were in training.

The answer came in a few days. The Monarchs offered him four hundred dollars a month, and Jackie packed his bags and headed for the Houston training camp.

The Monarchs put him at shortstop. From the first, it was apparent that his throwing arm left much to be desired in a shortstop. His pegs got to first base, but they lacked the snap and speed needed for the long throw from shortstop.

Still, he fielded well, he was fast and he got his glove in front of the ball. As spring training continued, it became evident, too, that he could hit, and he ran the bases like a demon.

Jackie might have been perfectly happy in Houston had he not been carrying out a troubling correspondence with Rachel. She had hoped Jackie would settle down in California after the Sam Houston College job, and that they could work out some kind of future together.

But this playing baseball with the Kansas City team. Where would it get him? She would hardly see him, what with their regular season and barnstorming tours later. And what would he have from it all? A couple of years of making fair money. Then what?

Well, a couple of years of making money was something he was willing to settle for right then, Jackie told Rachel. He'd be able to save some of it. And the war looked as though it would soon be over. Maybe things would change, there'd be new opportunities.

At any rate, he'd be no worse off than he was at Sam Houston, and he'd have some money in the meantime.

It was a battle for a while. Rachel didn't like the

idea at all. Neither did his mother. But he wasn't giving up that four hundred a month easily. What else could he do that would make him that much money?

Jackie won. Rachel and his mother reluctantly gave in.

Somehow, in retrospect, the controversy appears minor and ludicrous. For while the three of them argued, the mills of the baseball gods were ever grinding.

It was thirty-five years less a few months since Branch Rickey had sat in a darkening hotel room and listened to a Negro man cry.

It was getting to be the time. The time for the seed to emerge.

The phone rang in the clubhouse of the Monarchs' training camp at Houston. An attendant answered it, listened for a moment, then hurried out onto the playing field.

"Robinson!" he called. "Jackie Robinson! Long distance call for you, person to person."

Jackie's heart leaped. Rachel?

"From California?" he asked the attendant as he trotted in from the infield.

The man shook his head. "Pittsburgh. Fella name of Wendell Smith, from the Pittsburgh *Courier*."

CHAPTER SEVEN

J ACKIE ROBINSON stood off to the side of the batting practice cage at Boston's Fenway Park and tried to probe his emotions. He found he was more amused than annoyed. He had the feeling that the two Negro players standing there with him—Sam Jethroe of the Cleveland Buckeyes and Marvin Williams of the Philadelphia Stars—were experiencing the same amusement.

The three men were at Fenway Park for a tryout with the Boston Red Sox. What a joke, thought Jackie. The last thing in the world the Red Sox wanted was Negro ballplayers. But they had been pressured into giving the three Negroes a tryout and were going through the motions for appearances' sake.

Jackie hadn't even wanted to make the trip to Boston. But that phone call from Wendell Smith of the Pittsburgh *Courier* had persuaded him.

"Jackie," Smith had told him, "this is a chance to start the ball rolling. Sure, you're not going to make the Red Sox. But let's get some action going, some publicity about the possibility of us Negroes playing major league baseball. Break that wall of silence about the idea."

Robinson knew, as did Smith, that since the war began there had been mounting pressure against racial discrimination on all fronts—education, industry, sports, housing. The wartime theme was: if the Negro can die for his country, can't he live for it the same as a white person?

Many barriers were broken during the war, but the baseball world still did not yield. Now, in the spring of 1945, with the war in its final stages, the pressure on baseball mounted. Some white sports writers began to criticize baseball men for practicing discrimination.

Then, in Boston, city councilor Isadore Muchnick demanded that the Boston clubs—then both the Red Sox and the Braves—give Negroes a chance. If not, he threatened to sponsor a bill to outlaw baseball on Sunday.

Smith, the *Courier* sports writer, read about Muchnick's threat. He got in touch with the councilman and told him that he'd bring several worthwhile Negro players to Boston, if Muchnick would press for a tryout.

Muchnick agreed, and Smith rounded up Jethroe

and Williams. Then he called Robinson in Houston.

Jackie listened to Smith's story. He was convinced that the whole thing was a waste of time. He wasn't sure that Smith's idea of "getting the ball rolling" was even a good idea.

"Maybe we won't get the tryout," he said to the Pittsburgh newspaperman on the phone. "We'll look like darn fools. And worse, it'll look like we're trying to force the Sox to give us a tryout before they're ready to. Maybe the publicity will be bad, instead of good."

"You worried about being called a troublemaker, Robinson?" Smith asked.

He struck a nerve with that barb.

"Afraid!" Jackie stormed. "Smith, they've been calling me that since I was a kid in high school, because I stood up for my rights. And they'll be calling me a troublemaker all my life, if continuing to stand up for them makes me a troublemaker to some people.

"No, I'm not afraid of a little name-calling. If you think something will come of this so-called tryout, okay, count me in."

Jackie recalled his talk with Smith as he stood now in Fenway Park, and he wondered still about the wisdom of the long trip to Boston. The Monarchs weren't too happy about his going, either, but Smith had warned them:

"If word gets around that you wouldn't let Robinson off for a tryout with a major league team, you're going to look real great with the fans."

Well, here he was. He, Jethroe, and Williams, and about fifteen white youngsters. In the stands were councilman Muchnick, Wendell Smith, Red Sox manager Joe Cronin and general manager Eddie Collins.

On the field, conducting the workouts, was coach Hughie Duffy. At first the players, including the three Negroes, worked out on the field. Then they were given their chance to hit.

Williams was first man up. He hit the ball well, bouncing several line drives off the left field wall. Then up came Robinson.

Jackie set himself at the plate, relaxed with the knowledge that this was batting practice for nothing. And he rapped the ball all over Fenway Park. He hit to left and he hit to right. He stroked ball after ball off the left field fence.

The white players there for the tryout, all younger and less experienced, were visibly impressed with the Negroes' batting prowess. But the three men shrugged and laughed off the compliments.

After the workout, Duffy came over and handed the men application cards. "You guys did real good," the coach said to the three Negroes. "Fill out these cards and you'll be hearing from us."

That evening at dinner, Smith told the three men

he would now press for a tryout with the Braves. The players laughed.

"No, thanks," Jethroe said. "We had enough today. You hear that man say we'd hear from them? Man, if that don't beat all. We'll hear from the Red Sox like we'll hear from Adolf Hitler."

Robinson agreed. "Let's face it, Wendell. All the Red Sox or any team has to do is let us come out and hit a few and then say we're just not good enough. Who's going to say they're wrong? No, I'm heading right back for the Monarchs. The show's over here."

But the show wasn't over. It had started much earlier than any of the four Negroes sitting at the restaurant table realized. And it had, in fact, barely gotten up steam.

Two years earlier, when Branch Rickey had moved from the St. Lous Cardinals to the Brooklyn Dodgers, he had indicated rather casually to the Dodger directors that he was interested in someday bringing Negro players into the major leagues. A few eyebrows were raised, but no one voiced a protest.

In the spring of 1945, with the pressure mounting from political and social groups to introduce Negroes into baseball, Rickey felt the time had come to lead the way. It was time to erase the painful memory of Charley Thomas trying to scrape the skin off his hands.

Rickey felt one man was needed. One Negro player to open the door. But it would have to be one selected with great care. He would have to be better than the average player brought up from the minor leagues. More, he would have to possess a personality that would be acceptable to the white players and the public, and at the same time be able to withstand the most terrible of pressures against him.

It seemed a hopeless task. Where to find a man, white or Negro, to fulfill all that would be required of him? Rickey sighed and called in his scouts.

It would have been a wrong move, at that juncture, to send the scouts scurrying after a Negro to play with the Dodgers. The hullabaloo would have crippled the entire project. Instead, Rickey, that spring of 1945, organized the United States League, a new Negro baseball league that would be, the Dodger executive promised, a better organized affair than the current Negro leagues in operation.

Of course, this was Rickey's blind. The league never got off the ground, nor was it ever intended to. But now Rickey could call his scouts in and send them off to beat the bushes for Negro talent.

"You are to pay your own way into Negro league games," he instructed his men. "Go quietly, act unhurriedly, casually. If anyone asks, you are scouting talent for the new Brooklyn Brown Dodgers."

In addition to the part-time and local scouts Rickey had on his payroll all around the country, he sent out from the Dodgers' home office top talent spotters Clyde Sukeforth, Wid Matthews, Tom Greenwade and George Sisler.

The reports began to come in. Sukeforth had found a pitcher with a great fast ball. His name was Don Newcombe. There was a Cuban Negro around named Roy Campanella, a promising catcher. The Kansas City Monarchs had a good looking shortstop, Jackie Robinson.

Jackie Robinson. Jackie Robinson. The name began to pop up more and more. Now the reports snowballed into the Dodger offices on Montague Street—Jackie Robinson, Jackie Robinson. Runs like a thief. Will steal your glove if you'll let him. Hits good, has power, terrific bunter, tough to strike out. Not afraid to take with two strikes.

The fielding, though—covers ground, but arm not quite strong enough for shortstop.

Branch Rickey looked over every report on every man with a buzzard's eye. Robinson's name was by far the most frequently mentioned. Rickey buzzed for scout Tom Greenwade, handed him the reports on Robinson.

"Follow this Robinson," Rickey said, puffing energetically on the ever-present cigar in his mouth

"I want to know what you think. After every game, call me."

Greenwade called from half a dozen midwestern cities, as he followed the fast-traveling Monarchs.

"Robinson can bunt and run better than anybody I've ever seen," he reported. "And that includes the players in the major leagues right now. But his arm is weak. Maybe good enough for second base, but not for shortstop."

Rickey thought for a moment. "All right, Tom. Get off his trail now. I want Sisler to look at him."

Scout George Sisler was an expert on infielders. He sped to Chicago to catch the Monarchs' play, then returned to Rickey.

"Robinson could play second base for any team in the majors," he said.

Rickey's eyes glowed. He chewed his cigar stub viciously. Maybe . . . maybe. Suddenly his shaggy eyebrows narrowed in a frown. He looked up at Sisler.

"Then of course he's good enough to play with the Brown Dodgers," he said.

A smile flickered across Sisler's face. "Of course," he said. Sisler suspected there was more to this interest in Jackie Robinson than the "Brown Dodgers." At the same time, scout Tom Greenwade had also surmised Rickey's plans. Soon Clyde Sukeforth would begin to wonder, too.

Rickey grunted at Sisler's answer and waved the scout out of the office. Then he bent over the reports on his desk.

After a while he tilted his chair back and stared at the ceiling, eyes narrowed in thought. He pressed the tips of his fingers together and tapped them against each other. The blue smoke from his cigar curled upward and spread along the ceiling.

First, he must be right as a player, Rickey thought. Whoever he is, Robinson or anybody, he must first be good enough as a player. What was the use of a suitable personality if the ballplayer in the man couldn't make the major leagues? The whole thing would become academic.

No, that would never do. The man who would be chosen as the first Negro to try for the major leagues must make it—all the way. There must be absolutely no doubt about this. Anti-Negro elements would be eager enough to defeat the project. If the man turned out to be inferior in play, there would be enough "I-told-you-so's" to stretch around the world.

It would then be twice—no ten, fifty times as difficult to attempt the thing with a second player.

Rickey swung his chair forward to read the reports on Robinson again, though by this time he practically knew them by heart, word for word.

He reread the findings on Robinson's background. College man. All-around athlete. Good family. Didn't drink, didn't smoke. Had steady girl. Then came the part that disturbed Rickey.

Robinson had a reputation at college for being "belligerent, quick-tempered." He was known to talk back to officials, to fight vocally with other players. The report did say, however, that evidence pointed to this being a matter of color. Robinson, it was asserted, was considered by some whites an "uppity Negro."

Rickey considered this carefully. Quick-tempered. A delicate point. The shaggy eyebrows came together again in a thoughtful frown.

The cigar had gone out. Rickey relit the stub. He removed the cigar from his mouth and blew a cloud of smoke at the ceiling. Then he flipped the switch on the office intercom.

"Where's Sukeforth?" he barked.

Rickey listened a moment. "Tell him I want him. Right away."

He flipped the switch again and got out of his chair to pace the room. Back and forth across the office he strode, hands clasped behind his back, a cloud of blue smoke trailing him.

Sukeforth came in, started to sit down.

Rickey waved a hand at him.

"Don't sit down. Go pack your bags. Here's what I want you to do . . ."

CHAPTER EIGHT

W EARILY , Clyde Sukeforth squeezed himself into the narrow seat in the box behind the dugout of the Kansas City Monarchs. He removed his hat and mopped his perspiring face with a handkerchief. It was hot in Chicago in August. He looked out at the playing field of Comiskey Park and watched for a while as the Monarchs and the Chicago American Giants took their pregame practice. Then he looked at his score card, walked over to the railing alongside the Monarchs' dugout and called out to one of the players.

"Say, Robinson! Jackie Robinson!"

The Kansas City infielder, idly tossing the ball around along the first base line, looked over toward the dugout. He spotted the man waving at him, then shrugged and turned away. He couldn't stop right now to sign autographs.

"Robinson! Jackie Robinson!"

The man was still waving. Jackie frowned, hesitated, then trotted over to the railing.

59

The man put out his hand and introduced himself. "My name is Sukeforth. Clyde Sukeforth. I represent the Brooklyn Dodgers. I've been sent out here to scout you for the Brown Dodgers, for the new Negro league being formed."

Robinson smiled. "You came at a bad time, Mr. Sukeforth. I hurt my shoulder a couple of days ago, and I'm not going to be playing for at least a week."

Sukeforth sighed. What luck. Well, he still had a job to do. Rickey had told him in no uncertain terms what was expected.

"In that case," he said, "I might as well head back to my hotel and get some rest. How about meeting me there later and we can talk?"

Jackie hesitated. Something didn't sound right here. He couldn't quite put his finger on it, but . . . Anyway, who and what were the Brown Dodgers?

"What do we have to talk about?" he said to Sukeforth.

"About you, Brooklyn, the Brown Dodgers."

Robinson still hesitated.

"Look," Sukeforth said, "Branch Rickey didn't send me all the way out here to kid you or anything. I've been chasing around the country all summer scouting Negro talent, and now I'm here to see you. Isn't that simple enough?"

Robinson nodded. He still had a funny feeling, but this Sukeforth looked like a nice, honest guy.

60

"Okay," he said to the Dodger scout. "I'll come around after the game."

Later, in the coffee shop of the hotel, Sukeforth told him a little more. By now the Dodger scout was personally convinced that Rickey wanted Robinson for Brooklyn, all right. But for the major league Dodgers, not the Brown Dodgers. Of course, he gave no hint of this to Jackie.

"Listen," he said to the player, "maybe it's not such a bad thing that your shoulder is hurt right now. Leaving the team for a few days now won't bother them any."

Robinson looked at Sukeforth warily. "Leave them for what?"

"Well, Mr. Rickey wants you to come back to Brooklyn with me. He wants to talk to you."

"Come back to Brooklyn with you! I can't just pick myself up and leave the team to go to Brooklyn. What for?"

"All I know is," Sukeforth said gently, "Rickey sent me out here to bring you back to Brooklyn. We'll take care of all your expenses. And as I said, you're not playing anyway, so the Monarchs probably won't mind."

"No? And what if they do mind—and fire me?"

"Oh, I don't think they'd do that. Besides," Sukeforth smiled, "after you talk to Rickey, I don't think the Monarchs will matter to you any more."

Robinson looked up sharply. Thoughts flashed

through his mind. Was Sukeforth hinting at something? Or am I reading crazy things into what he just said? Anyway, it's probably true. The Monarchs wouldn't fire me if I took off for a few days, as long as I'm not playing.

"How much time do I have to think it over?" he asked the Dodger scout.

Sukeforth looked at his watch. "I figure we can catch the one o'clock train. That gives you about two hours to eat and pack." He was grinning at Robinson.

Jackie grinned back. "That's what I like. Plenty of time to make a decision." He shrugged. "Okay. What have I got to lose?"

"Nothing," Sukeforth assured him. "And plenty to gain."

The next afternoon Robinson, with Sukeforth at his side, stood in front of Branch Rickey.

The Dodger chief executive, after greeting Jackie cordially, sat silent, looking at the Negro player intently, as though he were trying to pierce the clothes and the skin to see what manner of man was underneath it all.

"Do you drink?" he asked suddenly.

Robinson started, surprised.

"No, I don't," he replied.

Rickey nodded. "Sit down," he said, kindly.

Jackie chose a chair. Sukeforth contented himself with leaning against a metal file cabinet.

Rickey nodded to himself again, then picked the stub of a cigar out of an ash tray, lit it, blew out the smoke and looked keenly at Robinson.

"You know what you're here for?"

"Well, Mr. Sukeforth here said you wanted to see me, something about these new Brown Dodgers you're organizing."

Rickey looked at Sukeforth, nodded, smiled.

"Those were his orders." He leaned over the desk. "Jackie, the fact is I'm interested in bringing you into the Brooklyn organization." He waited, But Robinson hadn't gotten the significance of the statement. Perhaps by "Brooklyn organization," he thought Rickey was still talking about the Brown Dodgers. So Rickey went on.

"Maybe Montreal to begin with . . ." He let his voice trail off.

Robinson looked up now. "Montreal!" He stared at Rickey, then at Sukeforth, who nodded, then back at Rickey.

The Dodger chief took out a fresh cigar. "Do you have a contract with the Monarchs?" he asked Robinson.

"No."

"Some kind of verbal agreement, then?"

"No. You just play, week to week, month to month."

"You think you can play for Montreal?"

Jackie gulped. "Yes."

Rickey turned quickly to Sukeforth. He looked at the scout and pointed to Robinson. "Can he do it?"

"He can run, he can field, he can hit," Sukeforth said quietly.

Rickey continued to look at the scout. Again the hand shot out, the finger pointed at Robinson.

"Has he got the guts?"

Robinson half rose from his chair. Then he sat down again. He looked at the two men. Sukeforth hadn't answered. Instead, he was looking at Robinson. Now Rickey, too, turned to look at Jackie.

Robinson wet his lips. "If you know anything about me, you know I've got guts," he said hoarsely.

Rickey charged out from behind the desk and stood towering over the seated ballplayer. His shaggy eyebrows shot up. "I know you've got a reputation as a troublemaker. A fighter. A hot-tempered player!" he shouted.

"I fight for my rights!" Robinson flared back.

"See! You're getting hot already!" Rickey snorted.

"If you're looking for a Negro who's going to cringe every time a white man says something to him, you got the wrong man, Mr. Rickey," Robinson said evenly. "I take plenty. But I won't let any man run over me."

"Why?" Rickey stormed. "To prove you've got guts? Boy, did you ever think that perhaps it requires more guts to take abuse without fighting back?"

Jackie hesitated. "I'm not so sure about that."

Rickey stomped back to his desk, ground his cigar stub in an ash tray. Then he sat down again in his leather armchair. He took a fresh cigar from its cellophane wrapper, lit it, blew the smoke in Robinson's direction.

"Well it does, boy, it does," he said finally. "Think about it a moment, and you'll find that when your immediate reaction to an insult is to strike back, it is the measure of your courage that you do not fight back."

"It still sounds like cowardice to me."

"No. Not necessarily," Rickey continued. "Listen to me, Jackie Robinson. We're trying a tremendous thing here. If you make good with Montreal, you will go right to the top. There will be no limits set on where you will play with the Brooklyn organization." Rickey let this sink in, then he went on.

"But you must realize what we all will face. I think you do realize it. Many, many people will be hoping you will fail, will be trying to *make* you fail. They know if you do, no one will try to bring a Negro into organized baseball for another ten, maybe another twenty years. Do you think you can succeed?"

"I'm sure I can play well enough to make the majors," Robinson said.

Rickey stood up. "But do you have guts enough to take what they will throw at you?"

Robinson set his jaw defiantly.

Rickey walked out from behind his desk. "They'll try to make you fight, don't you see? They'll try to start a riot in the ball park. They'll try to make it turn out so bad people will be afraid to come out to the park. Is that what you want?"

Jackie shook his head.

Rickey jabbed the cigar at him. "They'll spike you. They'll throw at your head. They'll call you every dirty name they can think of. And you won't be able to fight back."

Robinson nodded.

"Can you do it? Can you take it?" Rickey exclaimed. "You'll be fielding a ground ball and a white player will charge into you, knocking you to the ground. You'll get up ready to fight and he'll sneer at you, 'Next time get out of my way, you dirty black—'

"Are you strong enough to turn your back on him and walk away?"

"I can do it," Robinson said grimly.

"He'll shout after you that you're yellow, that all niggers are yellow. He'll curse your mother and your father. What will you do?"

Jackie's eyes blazed. "I'll let him yell. But he

better keep out of my way when *I'm* on the bases!"

"No!" Rickey shouted. "You do nothing! You've got to prove yourself with your hitting, your fielding and your running. And that is all!"

"How can I play that way? How can I be any good if I don't play hard?"

Rickey leaned over him. "You've got to do it that way. You can play hard baseball—and play clean. Get those hits that win games. Run the bases boldly, but cleanly. Field like my scouts say you can. But you've got to be deaf! Nerveless! *You've got to learn to take it!*"

Robinson sighed. "It'll be hard."

"Well, can you do it?" Rickey snapped.

"I can do it. I understand what's involved. It won't be easy. But it's a great opportunity you're giving me, Mr. Rickey. Too big to let it get away. I'll learn—I'll learn to turn the other cheek."

Rickey stalked back to his desk, sat down again wearily. He peered at Robinson sternly for a moment. Then he flicked the intercom switch.

"No more calls for the rest of the afternoon," Rickey barked. He turned back to Jackie.

"Do you have a girl, Jackie?" he asked mildly.

Robinson looked up, surprised.

"Why, yes, kind of," he replied.

Rickey's eyebrows flew up. "Kind of?"

"Well, yes. I do. But why? What does she have to do with all this?"

Rickey waved aside the questions.

"Marry her," he said. "Right away."

Jackie was bewildered by Rickey's sudden switch in conversation. "I still don't see—" he started, but Rickey broke in.

"It's the best thing for a young ballplayer. Steadies him. Don't wait, Jackie. When you get home, marry the girl. Now then," he continued, "let's get down to business."

Two hours later, Jackie walked out onto Montague Street. He felt a curious mixture of elation, confusion, fear and wonderment. Vaguely, too, he had the notion that something historic had just occurred, and that he was part of it.

He was proud, now, with his realization. He knew the burden that had been assigned him by Rickey. He was certain that he could live up to everything the Dodger executive expected of him. Rickey had given him the opportunity of a lifetime.

He would be the first. No matter what happened afterward, no matter how great any Negro player in baseball might ever be, this was something they could never take away from him. He would be the first Negro to play in organized baseball in the major leagues.

There was no doubt in Jackie's mind that he would eventually make the Dodgers. He was good enough, this he knew for certain.

But what a secret to keep! He recalled what

Rickey had told him a few minutes before in his office.

"This conversation must not get out," Rickey had cautioned him. "It would spoil everything to release this information to the press and the public prematurely."

And Jackie had shook his head. "I'll keep it quiet."

Rickey had smiled at that. "I don't want you to bust wide open, boy. Tell your mother, or tell your girl, but that's all. And you must impress on them the importance of their keeping your secret. I promise you that before the first of December you will be offered a contract to play with Montreal. Before that time, as far as anyone is concerned, you've been here to talk to me about the Brown Dodgers, and that's all."

The first of December. And this was August. Jackie felt the excitement rising in him as he walked down the steps of the subway that would take him to his Manhattan hotel. He hardly noticed the rush hour throngs that steamed past him, that pushed and jostled him in the packed train speeding through the dark of the underground to uptown Manhattan.

Jackie got off at his stop. Rachel! The name sprang to his mind. I'll have to call her first thing. His pace quickened as he neared the entrance to his hotel. He raced up the steps and pushed open the door to the lobby.

CHAPTER NINE

Branch Rickey had good reasons for wanting to delay the official signing and announcement of his great experiment with Jackie Robinson. First, he felt that the middle of the baseball season was bad timing for the triggering of the explosive situation. He preferred that Jackie break in with Montreal during the spring training season, and by announcing the news in January or February, he would be giving the players enough time to adjust to the idea—but not enough time to build up organized resistance.

In the second place, from a strictly publicity point of view, the middle of winter was a far better time; the sports pages are hungrier for news. Finally, there was still much groundwork to be done among the press, the players and the public before Rickey would be ready to let the Robinson secret out of the bag.

But Rickey wasn't the only one in New York

playing chess with the Negro-in-baseball question. The pressure groups were becoming increasingly active. Mayor LaGuardia, accordingly, had organized a Committee on Unity to study problems of race relationships, including the apparent discrimination against Negroes in baseball.

The mounting pressures, particularly from organizations seeking to profit politically by espousing the Negro cause, were dangerously close to blowing up into the "incident" stage.

Already, on opening day of the 1945 season, twenty Negroes had picketed the Yankee Stadium, representing a group called the End Jim Crow in Baseball Committee.

Soon after the incident, Dr. Dan W. Dodson, executive director of the Committee on Unity, wrote to Branch Rickey, and also to Larry MacPhail, then president of the New York Yankees, asking them to meet with him regarding the threatening racial situation.

Rickey checked into the background of Dr. Dodson. He discovered that Dodson was a sociology professor at New York University, and though born and bred in Texas he was a voluble supporter of integration. Two weeks later, the two men met in Rickey's office in Brooklyn.

The Dodgers president gestured Dodson to a chair and sat down behind his desk. Thoughtfully, he lit the ever-present cigar stub.

"Dr. Dodson," he said then, "I believe we can be of much mutual assistance." Rickey proceeded to outline briefly his scouting activities and his plan to introduce a Negro player into major league baseball. This was in June, before he'd decided on Robinson as the player.

"Now then," Rickey continued, "there are several problems involved which we can probably best solve together."

He lit a fresh cigar. "For one thing, we've got to stall those confounded pressure groups. Those people don't realize—or what's worse, they don't care about the consequences of moving too fast in this business."

Dr. Dodson smiled wryly. "There are elections to be won. The Negro vote, you know."

Rickey exploded. "Those darn fools! You can't just take any Negro ballplayer and throw him into the lions' den of white baseball! The wrong man, without proper preparation, will set the whole Negro cause back twenty years!"

"I agree," said Dodson. "And the mayor's committee doesn't seem to satisfy them. We'll need something stronger to hold them off."

"A new committee, maybe," Rickey said, "to deal directly with the problems of the Negro in baseball. Maybe that will hold these people off until I come up with the right man. I have several promising names I'm concentrating on now."

Dr. Dodson nodded. "That might be a good idea. We can get ten or more prominent citizens to serve on the committee, and we can announce to the press that we feel we're getting close to making a major stride in the direction of integrating Negroes into baseball. Without, of course, bringing you into the picture specifically."

"Well, maybe we can even get by without any such announcements," Rickey offered. "I wouldn't want anybody to put two and two together and figure out what I'm doing. Least of all the Negro players I'm scouting."

Dr. Dodson agreed.

"Now then," Rickey said, "I'll tell you what I think is the more important—and even tougher— problem. Handling the Negro people themselves."

Dodson looked at him inquiringly. "The Negro people?"

Rickey chewed vigorously on the cigar butt. "Yes, strangely enough, they might turn out to be their own worst enemies."

"How?" Dodson wanted to know.

Rickey removed the cigar and leaned across his desk. "Overenthusiasm."

Dodson studied the word for a moment. Then he nodded. "I think I see what you're driving at."

"Picture the situation," Rickey explained. "It's opening day. The first day a Negro player is to play in major league baseball. Thousands of justifiably enthusiastic Negro fans jam the park, parade through the stands happily, cause an uproar, maybe fights, race riots. And I don't believe I can exaggerate the possibilities."

"No, you do not," Dodson agreed. "The adulation and joy, justified, as you say, may easily get out of hand."

"Not only that," Rickey continued, "demonstrations would embarrass the player, make him press, affect his playing adversely. If his playing went off, and he had to be benched, picture the consequences of our not preparing the Negro public for such an eventuality."

Dodson shook his head. "Frankly, this side had not occurred to me. You paint a dark picture, but a true one nevertheless."

"Unfortunate," Rickey said, "but true, indeed."

"We'll have to map out a program of education," Dodson offered.

Rickey nodded. "A vast program, Dr. Dodson. Starting immediately. So that when I announce that I've found the player to be the first Negro of organized baseball, the entire Negro population of the country will be prepared—and will know how to act accordingly."

"A group of Negro leaders," Dodson pitched in, enthusiastic now. "Churchmen, educators, social workers, youth directors. We'll call in a small group here in New York, outline the program and have them spread it around the country."

"Exactly," Rickey nodded. "And we'll add the Negro press to that group. Restraint. Restraint will be our watchword. The Negro people must react with calm to this historic event. Any other course will arouse the resentment of the white fans."

Dr. Dodson stood up and paced the room. "No demonstrations of any kind. No organized rooting sections, no whooping and hollering." He turned and faced Rickey. "You realize how mucn we're asking?"

Rickey laughed shortly. "You realize what we're asking of the man who'll bear the brunt of all this? You know what he's going to have to face on the field, from the players and hostile fans?"

Dr. Dodson sighed. "We've got our work cut out, all right."

Forming the new committee to stall the pressure groups was the first item on the agenda for the two men. It wasn't easy; most of the prominent citizens they approached weren't interested or had "no time" to serve. Only pressure exerted by Mayor La-Guardia finally swung enough influential citizens into serving on the committee.

Temporarily, most of the pressure groups were mollified, and another threatened demonstration, this time at the Polo Grounds, was averted.

Soon, however, the pressure and the tumult rose

again. The Negro in baseball was becoming the political football of the year. A group representing the governor of New York State asked that the three New York clubs sign a nondiscrimination pledge. They refused.

Then Mayor LaGuardia, in whose name the committee to study the integration problem was formed, decided he should make more capital of that fact. In his Sunday broadcasts to the people of New York City, he talked about how "his" committee would bring Negroes into baseball.

By this time Rickey had talked with Robinson. He had decided to wait until winter to sign Robinson to an official contract. Jackie, in the meantime, had gone back home to California. At first he'd returned to the Monarchs, intending to play out the season. But they told him he'd have to continue with the team right through a barnstorming tour afterward, or not at all. Jackie chose not at all. He felt he needed a long rest before embarking on his venture into organized baseball.

Now Rickey was backed into a corner. The situation was rapidly deteriorating. Rickey wasn't quite ready to spring Robinson on the public. But . . .

Then in October Mayor LaGuardia contacted Rickey. He wanted to be able to announce, on his forthcoming Sunday broadcast, that as a result of the mayor's Committee on Unity, baseball would shortly begin to sign Negro players.

That threw the political football right in Rickey's lap. Only Rickey didn't want to play. Instead, he wired Robinson to come east at once, to fly directly to Montreal and meet him on the morning of October 23rd in the offices of the Montreal Royals. Then Rickey got busy on the telephone.

The morning of the twenty-third, sports writers for the Montreal papers and wire services were alerted to a press conference in the Royals' office. The writers were completely in the dark about the nature of the conference.

As they trooped into the office, they found waiting there Hector Racine, president of the Montreal Royals, Colonel Romeo Gauvreau, vice-president of the club, Branch Rickey, Jr., son of the Dodger president and director of the Brooklyn farm clubs, and Jackie Robinson.

Racine dropped the bombshell without preliminaries. "Gentlemen," he began, dropping his arm on Jackie's shoulder, "this is Jackie Robinson, a shortstop. He has just been signed to play for the Montreal club for the 1946 season."

Running like a pack of frightened geese, the reporters headed for the telephones.

CHAPTER TEN

REACTION to the signing of Jackie Robinson was immediate and loud. On the whole, baseball men tended to be wary of their comments, lest they be accused of outright race prejudice. However, some were less concerned with tact than they were with the possibility of a Negro playing major league baseball.

One of the more outspoken was the late W. G. Bramham, then the commissioner of minor league baseball. Quoted in the Durham, North Carolina, *Herald,* Bramham let loose at Branch Rickey.

"Whenever I hear a white man, whether he be from the North, South, East or West, broadcasting what a Moses he is to the Negro race, right then I know the latter needs a bodyguard," the commissioner said.

"It is those of the carpetbagger stripe of the white race," he went on, "who, under the guise of helping but in truth using the Negro for their own selfish interest, retard the race . . .

"Father Divine will have to look to his laurels, for we can expect Rickey Temple to be in the course of construction in Harlem soon."

Bramham admitted, however, that there was nothing he could do about the situation. There was no law forbidding the signing of Negro players.

An official protest did come from a surprising source. As soon as the news hit the wires that Robinson had been signed by Montreal, T. Y. Baird, part owner of the Kansas City Monarchs, declared that he would file a protest with Commissioner Albert "Happy" Chandler.

"Robinson signed a contract with us last year," Baird said, "and he is Kansas City property. If Commissioner Chandler lets Rickey get away with this, he's really starting a mess."

Jackie, who had previously denied to Branch Rickey the existence of a contract, again denied that he had any written agreement with the Monarchs. Nor was the existence of such a contract proved by the Monarchs.

The legality of the situation was apparently also the prime concern of Clark Griffith, the Washington Senators' owner. "The only question that occurs to me," Griffith told a reporter, "is whether organized baseball has a right to sign a player from a Negro league."

This tack was taken by many baseball men, with varying reasons. Some were sincere, perhaps, in their regard for the health of the Negro leagues. However, more were using the protest as a front for their prejudice, or for reasons of a financial interest in Negro league baseball. For it was obvious that if the Robinson experiment were a success, there would no longer be a need for Negro baseball.

Branch Rickey answered all of these protests in one statement to the press. "There is no Negro league as such as far as I'm concerned," Rickey said. "Negro baseball is in the zone of a racket and there is not a circuit that could be admitted to organized baseball . . ."

Three days after Robinson signed with Montreal, the owners of the Kansas City Monarchs, T. Y. Baird and J. L. Wilkinson, withdrew their earlier protest. Baird, who had been the spokesman for the partners, telegraphed Rickey that he had been misquoted and misinterpreted.

". . . would not do anything to hamper or impede the advancement of any Negro ballplayer, nor would we do anything to keep any Negro ballplayer out of white major leagues," the telegram read.

It was probable that the Monarchs' owners had been advised that a fight with Rickey would not sit well with the Negro people, who were overjoyed with the news that a Negro was getting a chance to play in organized baseball. Both Baird and Wilkinson are white.

In the meantime, reporters were scurrying to the four corners of the country, getting the reaction from anybody who cared to be quoted. They asked baseball men, the man on the street, businessmen, religious leaders, sociologists. Most people willing to be quoted were cautious in their statements.

Frank Shaughnessy, then president of the International League, told the Associated Press:

"There's no rule in baseball that says a Negro can't play with a club in organized ball. As long as any fellow's the right type and can make good and get along with other players, he can play ball. I don't think much prejudice exists any longer. I believe such things are more political than social now."

William Benswanger, president of the Pittsburgh Pirates in 1945, dismissed the matter in a sentence. "It is the affair of the Brooklyn and Montreal clubs whom they may sign, whether white or colored."

Jack Horner, who had interviewed Commissioner Bramham for the Durham *Herald,* concluded that the experiment was doomed to failure. "The general impression in this city," Horner wrote, "is that the Negro player will be so uncomfortable, embarrassed and out of place in organized baseball that he will soon get out of his own accord."

President Alvin Gardner of the Texas League

was even more certain. "I'm positive you'll never see any Negro players on any of the teams in organized baseball in the South as long as the Jim Crow laws are in force."

Baseball Commissioner Happy Chandler refused to comment. "I have nothing to say either way," he told reporters.

With several notable exceptions, the baseball writers covering the major leagues applauded Rickey. Many had been campaigning for the Negro to play in organized ball. Dan Parker of the New York *Daily Mirror,* Bill Corum of the New York *Journal-American* and Red Smith, then with the Philadelphia *Record* and now with the New York *Herald Tribune,* were three notably consistent campaigners.

When Montreal signed Robinson, these men were loud in their support. Though Corum doubted that Robinson could ever make the Dodgers because of his age—Jackie was twenty-six, old for a minor league rookie—he thought it was about time baseball gave Negroes their due.

"To make a *cause célèbre* of the matter, to stir a tempest in a teapot, can do nothing or nobody, including the Negro race, baseball, Chandler, the Rickeys and in the end, most important of all, our country, anything but harm . . .

"Members of all races and from all sorts of places have been meeting together in the (boxing) ring on the may-the-best-man-win basis for so long that people with any sense at all have ceased to give it a second thought.

"It won't be many years until the same will be true of Negroes playing in organized baseball. Someday the big leagues (though it is doubtful if Robinson at twenty-six can climb up the hill) must be that way if the National Pastime is to continue to be a sport in sports-loving America."

Columnist Smith said in the Philadelphia *Record:* ". . . Since the Montreal Club, a Brooklyn farm, overstepped baseball's unwritten Jim Crow policy by signing Jackie Robinson, a Negro infielder, there has been a fancy assortment of public statements of baseball men.

"Consider the views expressed, starting with that of Washington's Clark Griffith. Now that positive action has been taken, Griff suddenly emerges as the defender of the American Negro league's property rights. It is not on record that Griff ever concerned himself with the property rights of the Cuban and South American teams whence he drew material.

"If Robinson has the guts and ability to stick it out until he can win acceptance in all quarters outside of baseball, he'll have no difficulties in the clubhouse. There is more democracy in the locker room than on the street . . ."

Almost needless to say, the attitudes of Corum and Smith were not unanimous.

The St. Louis *Sporting News,* which is to baseball what *Variety* is to show business, held little hope for Robinson's success.

"Robinson, at twenty-six," the newspaper said, "is reported to possess baseball abilities which, were he white, would make him eligible for a trial with, let us say, the Brooklyn Dodgers' Class B farm at Newport News, if he were six years younger.

"He is . . . placed in competition with a vast number of younger, more skilled and more experienced players. This factor alone appears likely to beat him down."

Jimmy Powers of the New York *Daily News* was another who predicted Robinson would fail.

"Jackie Robinson, the Negro signed by Brooklyn, will not make the grade in the big leagues next year or the next . . . Every major league ball club has a backlog of young talent, proven stars, returning from the war.

"Robinson would have to be a super player to 'bump' a returning veteran. We would like to see him make good, but . . . Robinson is a 1000–1 shot to make the grade."

Most of the ballplayers questioned, particularly those on the Dodgers, were noncommittal, refusing to go out on a limb that might someday be sawed off behind them.

Dodger outfielder Fred "Dixie" Walker, known colloquially as "The People's Cherce" because of his immense popularity with Brooklyn fans, summed up that attitude.

"As long as he isn't with the Dodgers," the southern-born Walker declared, "I'm not worried."

However, Rogers Hornsby, baseball immortal from Texas, thought Rickey had made a mistake.

"The way things are," Hornsby said, "it will be tough for a Negro player to become part of a close-knit group such as an organized ball club. Ballplayers on the road have to live close together . . . I think Branch Rickey was wrong in signing Robinson to play with Montreal—it won't work out."

Back in California, meanwhile, Robinson wasn't playing ostrich. He was reading the comments in the newspapers, favorable and unfavorable, filing them mentally for future reference. When he got up to the Dodgers—and Jackie was confident he would get there—he thought it would be a good idea to recall who had been for him, who against.

With confidence in his future, and the blessings of Branch Rickey, Jackie at last married Rachel Isum, on February 10, 1946 in the same Methodist church the Robinsons had been attending since they moved to Pasadena.

Two weeks later, the Robinsons were bound for Daytona Beach, Florida, where the Dodgers and their farm teams were to be taking spring training. They started by plane from Los Angeles, but in New Orleans they were "bumped" by an army priority.

So from New Orleans they went by a train to Jacksonville. At Jacksonville they were informed they'd have to go the rest of the way by bus.

The bus, of course, was Jim Crow. There were reclining seats in the front and center sections, straight-backed hard seats in the rear, where Negroes were supposed to sit.

Jackie and Rachel boarded the bus for the sixteen-hour trip, found it half empty and settled wearily in the reclining seats in the center of the bus. Since they'd lived most of their lives in Pasadena, they weren't in the habit of reacting to—or immediately recognizing—every Jim Crow situation. They were quickly enlightened, however.

The bus driver turned, frowned and motioned silently for them to get into the rear sections. Resignedly, Jackie and Rachel moved to the straight seats in the rear. They rode that way for sixteen hours. Along the way, the driver told them they could eat by going to the back door of the restaurants at which the bus stopped.

The Robinsons preferred not to eat at all.

As the bus pulled into Daytona Beach at last, Jackie and Rachel looked anxiously at each other. The same thought was in both their minds. The incidents during the trip from California had brought the point home to them clearly.

The honeymoon was over. The test was about to begin.

CHAPTER ELEVEN

THE air was crisp and alive over Jersey City that eighteenth day of April, 1946. And in Roosevelt Stadium it fairly crackled with excitement. It was opening day, Montreal against Jersey City. But it was more than that.

Thirty-five thousand fans had jammed the stadium to witness the debut of Jackie Robinson, the first Negro in organized baseball. They had read about his exploits all during the spring training season. They had read of the controversy surrounding his playing in the militantly anti-Negro sections of the South. Now they had come in swarms to see the phenomenon in the flesh, expecting anything to happen, hoping for they didn't know what.

Roosevelt Stadium was like the scene of a giant carnival. Or perhaps a great bullfight or an ancient Roman arena. Only it was Jackie Robinson, instead of the Christians, being thrown to the lions.

Whatever it was, they had come from miles around to witness the exhibition. They had come prepared to cheer and to jeer, to shout and to scream and argue with their neighbors in the surrounding seats. They had paid their way in, and by heavens, they were going to get their money's worth.

In the Montreal dugout, Jackie Robinson stood silently, one foot on the top step, and looked out over the stadium. He could feel his heart pounding in his chest.

They're here to look at me, he thought without vanity. They're here to see the freak perform. Occasionally, from a distance, he could hear his name being called, as a fan in the stands would notice him. Well, he thought, maybe I'm being a little unfair. Probably some of these people are really pulling for me to make it.

The umpires called time. Thirty-five thousand fans leaped to their feet and roared as one voice as the Jersey City Giants trotted out to their positions on the field. Mayor Frank Hague of Jersey City marched out to the flagpole with a squad of dignitaries for the traditional opening day flag-raising ceremonies.

The flag of the United States of America rose slowly to the top of the pole. Then the band struck up "The Star-Spangled Banner." Robinson, standing in the dugout, his head bared, felt the lump rise in his throat as he sang the words: ". . . o'er the land of the free and the home of the brave."

And as the first Montreal player walked up to bat, Robinson thought back to all that had happened to him that spring.

When he and Rachel stepped off the bus at Daytona Beach, after that backbreaking sixteen-hour ride, they were met by Wendell Smith, the Pittsburgh *Courier* sports editor, and the paper's photographer Billy Rowe. The two men had gone down in advance to arrange housing accommodations for Jackie and his wife. They could not, of course, be quartered with the rest of the Montreal players and their families.

Smith had arranged for the Robinsons to stay with a prominent Negro family, along with pitcher Johnny Wright, another Negro whom Rickey had signed shortly after Robinson.

The following morning Robinson and Wright drove over to the Montreal training site, which was about twenty miles south of Daytona Beach, at Sanford. They walked out onto the playing field hesitantly, half fearful, not actually expecting anything, yet not knowing what to expect. There were more than a hundred players on the field, tossing baseballs around, hitting fungoes, chasing fly balls. Robinson and Wright suddenly felt all alone, naked, standing there on the field, knowing that the other players were eying them curiously.

Finally Jackie saw a familiar, smiling face. Clyde Sukeforth was coming their way, his hand outstretched in welcome. "Hop into the dressing room and get your uniforms," he said to the two men. "Babe Hamberger's been expecting you."

When they had dressed, Sukeforth introduced them to Clay Hopper, the Mississippi-born Montreal manager. Hopper, speaking quietly with a soft drawl, shook hands with the two men and related briefly what they were to do their first couple of days in training.

His voice and his attitude betrayed nothing of his feelings toward Robinson and Wright. Both men knew that Hopper was fighting a dramatic battle with himself.

The first several days of training passed without incident. The Montreal regulars and the men trying out tended to be cool, but not hostile. Robinson and Wright minded their own business, didn't speak unless spoken to—and worked hard.

Jackie worked too hard, in fact. In his eagerness to impress Hopper and his future teammates, Jackie played in the intrasquad practice games as though he were in midseason condition. He inevitably came up with a sore arm.

One evening Robinson and Wright returned from

the playing field to find Smith and Rowe of the *Courier* waiting for them.

"Pack your stuff, fellows, and let's get going," Smith said tightly.

"Going?" Robinson asked. "Where?"

"Back to Daytona. Right away."

"What are you talking about? We've got a couple of more days of training here in Sanford before we move on to Daytona," Jackie said.

"Has something happened? We been dropped from the team—or what?"

Smith and Rowe looked at each other grimly.

"Something's happened, all right," Rowe said. "You've been given the bum's rush out of Sanford, that's what. You've been ordered to get out of town, fast. They won't stand for Negro players on the same field with white men. We're going back to Daytona."

At Daytona, when the Royals moved there several days later, Hopper shifted Robinson to second base. It was known from the beginning that his arm wouldn't do for a shortstop, and now, with Jackie's shoulder sore, the Montreal manager moved him to where the throws wouldn't be as difficult.

Although the position was new to Robinson, his great natural ability, coupled with help from a teammate, named Lou Rochelli, soon had him fielding brilliantly.

While Montreal remained in Daytona Beach,

there were no racial incidents. But when the Royals had to play on exhibition elsewhere, they ran into trouble. In Jacksonville they were scheduled to play against the Jersey City Giants. When the team got to the field, they found the gate padlocked. A muttering crowd was waiting outside.

"What's going on?" Manager Hopper asked one of the fans.

"Game's been called off, we hear," the man said. "They ain't gonna let you on the field with niggers on your team."

In De Land, Florida, in an exhibition game against Indianapolis, Jackie suffered the embarrassment of being thrown off the field while the game was in progress. He had just slid home with a run when a man with a sheriff's badge walked out onto the field and grabbed him by the collar.

"You git off this field right now or I'll throw you in jail," the sheriff declared. "We ain't havin' no nigras playin' on the same field with white boys."

Jackie's immediate reaction was a decision to quit, to pack his bags and get Rachel and go back to California. Who needs this? he reflected bitterly. Why subject myself to this kind of abuse?

But then he realized that this was exactly what those who were against him wanted him to do, were trying to make him do. Quit. He gritted his teeth and played on.

As the Montreal Royals wound their way northward during the exhibition season, they continued to meet with resistance from local authorities. In Augusta, in Savannah, in Greensboro, in Richmond, their games were canceled, the stadiums padlocked.

By this time Jackie had become reconciled to such action. To his pleasant surprise, however, he had found that when Montreal was allowed to play, there was little hostility from the fans or the opposition ballplayers. True, there were jeers and racial slurs from some sections of the grandstand when he appeared on the field, but these were more than outweighed by the sincere applause he often was accorded, even from gatherings of southerners.

More than once he had heard the encouraging shout from a box seat, "Come on, black boy! They're givin' you a chance—let's see you do somethin' about it!"

Well, here was his chance now. Opening day. He kneeled in the "on deck" circle in front of the Royals' dugout, watching as Montreal's lead-off hitter shortstop Stan Breard worked the count to two and two, then bounced out to the shortstop.

Jackie took a deep breath and walked into the batter's box, swinging a pair of bats. He threw the specially weighted one away and set himself at the plate. From the stands had come a great shout as the public address system announced his name; now there was a hush over the playing field.

He could hear the calls from his teammates in the dugout, encouraging him. "Get a hold of one, Jackie!"

He moistened his lips and waited for the first pitch. It was in for a strike. The next serve was outside for a ball. Jackie felt rooted to the spot. The bat was a ton on his shoulder. He took a strike, then another ball. He was overcome by a kind of paralysis. He couldn't swing. The next pitch was high. Three balls and two strikes.

Jackie stepped out of the box. He stooped and rubbed some dirt on his hands. His head was buzzing with sound. The field was a blur. He shook his head to clear it. Then he stepped back in. Three and two. He mustn't strike out! Not with the bat on his shoulder!

The pitch came in. Jackie lunged at it, trickled the ball slowly out to shortstop. The Giants' infielder scooped it up and easily threw Jackie out at first base.

In the second inning the Royals had a rally going and Jackie got his second chance to bat. On base were Tom Tatum and George Shuba. Jackie watched the first two pitches sail by for a ball and a strike. The initial tension was gone now. He was watching the pitches calmly, instead of frozenly.

Again the count went to three and two. Jackie glanced down at the third base coach to see if the hit-and-run sign was on. Then he leaned into the plate, cocked his bat. The pitch came down.

Jackie swung—and he felt the clean crack of wood against horsehide as his bat met the ball squarely. He raced madly down the first base line. The crowd was roaring. As he made his turn at first he saw the ball disappear into the left field stands, saw the umpire pinwheel his right arm to signal a home run.

His heart swelling with joy and pride, Jackie trotted around the rest of the bases. Roosevelt Stadium resounded with shouts and applause. Shuba and Tatum waited at home plate to shake Robinson's hand as he tallied the first home run of his career in organized baseball.

But Jackie was just getting warmed up. The shackles were off him now. He was feeling loose and at ease. In the fifth inning he bunted and caught the third baseman asleep. He beat it out easily. Then, on the second pitch to the next batter, he stole second. The batter grounded out and Jackie went to third.

As the Giants' hurler began his windup for the first pitch to the next Montreal batter, Jackie bluffed a run for the plate. Halfway down the line he stopped. The catcher threw to third but Jackie slid back ahead of the tag.

Again he danced off, threatening to steal home, jockeying back and forth down the third base line.

The Jersey City pitcher threw to third, but Robinson was back. He led off the bag again, and again the pitcher threw to hold him on. The fans began to hoot now at the Jersey City hurler.

Jackie grinned. This guy's getting rattled now, he thought. On the next pitch I'm going. He extended his lead. The Giants' pitcher looked over at him, wound up—and Jackie took off full steam for the plate. The pitcher looked at him in panic, hesitated, started to throw to the plate, stopped, then finally just stood there looking foolish. By not completing his motion, the pitcher had committed a balk.

The plate umpire waved a grinning Robinson across the plate to score.

In the seventh inning, Jackie singled and again stole second. The next batter singled and Robinson scored his third run of the day. In the eighth, Jackie singled for his fourth straight hit. Another hit moved him to third. The dance along the third base line was started once more. A different pitcher was on the mound for Jersey City, but the result was the same.

Jackie so upset the hurler that he, too, balked. For the second time that day, Jackie got a free ride home.

Montreal won the game, 14–1. In his first game of organized ball, Jackie battled in four runs on four hits, scored four times and stole two bases.

The fans overran the field after the game, chasing Robinson for autographs. If there had been any doubt about it before, there was none now. Robinson was good enough to play for Montreal.

The International League itinerary for the Royals included Toronto, Baltimore, Syracuse, Newark, Jersey City, Buffalo and Rochester. Only in Baltimore did Jackie find segregation ordinances, and only with the Syracuse team did he experience anything other than normal bench jockeying.

Before Montreal's first visit to Baltimore, Branch Rickey had been warned by International League president Frank Shaughnessy that Robinson was in physical danger if he dared show up in uniform in the Baltimore park.

Rickey just waved his cigar and dismissed the warnings.

Shaughnessy showed Rickey clippings from Baltimore newspapers predicting rioting should Robinson attempt to play.

"There won't be any trouble," Rickey assured the distraught Shaughnessy. "All these people ever do is shout threats of dire happenings. Nothing will happen. Robinson will play for his team in Baltimore."

Rickey was right. Except for more than the usual amount of jeering from the stands, there were no incidents. And in Baltimore, too, Jackie found the only city that forbade him to stay at the hotel with his teammates.

The abuse heaped upon Jackie from the Syracuse team was a more serious problem. During each game, the men on the bench would hold aloft black cats and shout at Jackie.

"Hey, Robinson, here's a couple more of your relatives!"

Jackie's only answer was to play a little harder against Syracuse.

In his home city of Montreal, Jackie was met by complete acceptance. Negroes, in truth, were practically unknown in the Canadian city. There was no tradition of slavery, intolerance and segregation; no racial friction. Their neighbors regarded the Robinsons as curiosities, and in that baseball-minded city Jackie quickly became one of the most popular members of the team.

After the first month of play, the season's pattern was established. Robinson was leading the league in hitting, he was fielding masterfully, he was running wild on the base paths.

And Montreal was well on its way to the pennant.

In August, Jackie's playing suddenly tailed off. But Montreal was so far ahead it clinched the pennant before the month was out. The team doctor, concerned about Robinson's sudden listlessness, had him undergo a complete examination.

"You're on the verge of a complete nervous breakdown," Jackie was told. "You've been under the severest mental and physical pressure for nearly a year. You can't take much more of it. Get away from baseball for at least a week. Don't even read a paper or listen to a radio. Either that, or you'll collapse at any moment."

For ten days Jackie stayed away from baseball. Then he returned, strong and refreshed, to win the batting championship of the International League.

He hit .349 in winning the title, tied for the lead in runs scored with 113, led second basemen in fielding with a .985 average, and stole 40 bases, second in the league to teammate Marv Rackley's 65.

The Little World Series was next, Montreal against Louisville, champs of the American Association. Louisville, Kentucky, where no Negro had ever played ball in competition with white men.

The Louisville fans rode the Montreal team mercilessly and Jackie most cruelly of all. They poured forth torrents of abuse, jeered all the louder as Montreal dropped two out of three games at Louisville. Jackie got but one hit in the three games.

When the series switched to friendly Montreal, Robinson and the Royals came to life. Jackie hit like a demon and he was a revelation on the bases. He finished the series, despite his poor start, with a .333 average. Montreal swept three in a row at home to win the championship, and Jackie himself scored the winning run in the final game.

The demonstration that followed that final game has never been equaled in Montreal sports history. Overjoyed Montreal citizens swarmed over the field. They grabbed Robinson, winning pitcher Curt Davis and Clay Hopper, the manager, and lifted the three men to their shoulders. For half an hour the celebrants paraded around the field, singing and dancing, carrying the three with them.

Finally, with the aid of park police, Robinson dashed into the clubhouse. There he was mobbed again, this time by his teammates. And Clay Hopper, the manager from Mississippi, came over to Jackie and extended his hand.

"You're a great ballplayer and a fine gentleman," he said.

Jackie dressed hurriedly and rushed to the street. But outside the park he was met again by a chanting, cheering crowd of Canadians. They pressed him for autographs, they tore at his clothing, they shouted his name.

Robinson tried to bull his way through the crowd. "I have to get to my hotel," he cried to the crowd.

"To the hotel!" the crowd took up the cry.

They lifted Jackie once again to their shoulders and began to march down the street. And Jackie sat there above the cheering crowd, lips grinning and the tears running unashamedly down his cheeks, as his friends bore him in triumph through the streets of Montreal.

CHAPTER TWELVE

THE tree had borne its fruit. It but remained now to be presented to the public. After Jackie Robinson's sensational season with Montreal, there were few men in baseball who doubted that he would be brought up to the Brooklyn Dodgers for the 1947 campaign. Everyone waited for Rickey's announcement of the transfer.

But the Dodger president wasn't ready. He was still unsure of the Dodger players' feelings about Robinson. There were, he knew, vague undercurrents of uneasiness, particularly among several of the players with southern backgrounds.

Rickey devised a two-way plan to ease Robinson's ascension to the Dodgers. First, he scheduled the Brooklyn and Montreal spring training program for Cuba and Panama. After the experiences in Florida and other southern states the previous year, training there again with Negroes on the squad was out of the question. In Cuba and Panama, the Dodgers would get to play exhibitions against teams which were predominantly Negro, in this way becoming accustomed to the presence of Negro players.

Rickey's second idea was that the actual suggestion that Robinson should be brought up to the Dodgers would come from Manager Leo Durocher. Rickey reasoned that after a Dodger-Montreal exhibition series, in which Robinson, if he were up to form, would star for the Royals, the voluble Durocher would start squawking that he wanted and needed Jackie.

It didn't work out that well.

Spring training began in Havana. The Dodgers were quartered in the luxurious Hotel Nacional, and Montreal at the Havana Military Academy. All of Montreal—that is, except Jackie Robinson and three other Negro players signed by Rickey.

Johnny Wright, who had been tried out at Montreal the year before with Robinson, hadn't made the grade. But now Rickey had three more Negroes who looked promising—Roy Campanella, a catcher, and pitchers Roy Partlow and Don Newcombe.

These four were assigned to a hotel in midtown Havana. It was a depressing-looking hotel, fronting on a narrow, noisy, dirty street. The lobby was dark and stale with the smoke of cheap cigars, and discarded butts littered the floor. An open-faced, creaky elevator brought the players up to their rooms.

After a couple of weeks in Havana, the Dodgers flew to Panama for a series of exhibitions; the Royals were to follow in a few days. In the meantime, there had been no word from Rickey about Robinson. Jackie continued to work out at second base, wondering what was going to happen to him, whether anything was going to happen at all.

Back in Brooklyn, Rickey was chewing cigars to shreds. In addition to the other problems surrounding Robinson, there was a new one that had come to mind. The Dodgers had an excellent shortstop—second base combination in Pee Wee Reese and Eddie Stanky. At the moment, frankly, there was no room for Robinson at second.

The Dodger president pondered this, smoking cigars in an endless chain until his office was blue with smoke. He spent hours on the telephone checking with his aides. Finally he came to a decision.

When Montreal checked into the Camp Clayton Army Base in Panama several days later, Jackie Robinson found a first baseman's mitt waiting for him.

"It's Rickey's idea, not mine," Manager Hopper told the indignant Robinson. "I don't like the idea myself, Jackie. We don't need you at first base.

Maybe Rickey wants you to break in to play first with the Dodgers, I don't know."

"Then why doesn't he have me working out with the Dodgers, instead of here?" Jackie asked.

Hopper shrugged. "I just work here, Jackie, same as you. Something's up, I know, because we sure don't need you at first in Montreal." The puzzled manager spread his hands resignedly. "Well, we'll know soon enough. Rickey doesn't do anything without a good reason."

Hopper was right about that. The Dodger boss had decided that first base was the only logical spot for Robinson to play if he was to come up to Brooklyn that year. The Dodgers had Howie Schultz and Eddie Stevens alternating at the bag the year before, neither with notable success. The Dodger players themselves would rebel less against Jackie breaking in at first than in any other infield position.

However, when the Royals arrived in Panama for their exhibition games with the parent club, the presence of Robinson at first base immediately tipped off the Dodger players that Rickey had him slated to join them when the regular season opened.

The strong anti-Negro element among the Dodgers began to make its move. They circulated among the players, those they knew were either undecided about Robinson or mildly anti-Negro, with the intention of drawing up a petition of protest.

Word of the move trickled to Jackie. Of course, he had expected some resentment, some rebelliousness, but he was nevertheless hurt and bitter.

One morning, sitting alone on his cot in the barracks building at Camp Clayton where the Dodgers were quartered, Jackie was visited by sports writer Herb Goren, then with the New York *Sun,* and now publicity director of the New York Rangers hockey team.

Goren, a Robinson supporter from the first, did not mention that he knew of the petition to keep Jackie off the Dodgers. Robinson was not so reticent.

"I hear the Dodgers don't want me," he blurted. "They say I might be a morale problem. Well, if that's the way they feel, I don't want to impose myself upon them. I'll stay with Montreal. I was no problem there. We won the pennant and the Little World Series. The ball club liked me and I liked them. And the people in Montreal liked me and I liked them, too."

Goren was stunned. Robinson, under Rickey's orders, had avoided offering his thoughts or opinions about anything, and particularly about his personal situation. Never before had Jackie been so outspoken with a reporter.

"You mean you'd be perfectly willing to go back with Montreal?" Goren asked.

Robinson's eyes blazed with anger. "Why not? They paid me pretty good. Sure, I want to move up to the Dodgers, but only because I've got a wife, and a kid now, too, to provide for. I could use the extra money. I'm not in baseball to start something. I just want to make a decent living for my family, and this is as good a way as any."

Word of the petition reached Branch Rickey, who had joined the two teams in Panama several days earlier. The Dodger chief moved quickly to pinch off the rebellion. He was seething with anger, but even in that emotional condition Rickey was wise enough to attack with care.

He vented his wrath on the borderline Dodgers, those who were neither anti-Negro nor particularly pro, but who had allowed themselves to be swayed into joining the petitioners. He called them into his office, one by one, and stormed at them for their unfairness, their un-Americanism and their stupidity; then he kicked them out of his office.

Those players who had strong anti-Negro feelings he handled differently. Rickey realized that these men had lived all their lives in a segregationist, anti-Negro atmosphere. He knew any attempt to browbeat them into line would make things worse for Jackie.

He told them simply that their objections to Robinson would not prevent him from transferring Jackie to the Dodgers. He asked them to try to play with Robinson, to see if their feelings would perhaps change. If not, Rickey said, he would arrange to have them traded to another team.

There were two Dodger players in particular— both from the South—with whom Rickey had the most difficulty. They were catcher Bobby Bragan, and the popular outfielder Dixie Walker.

Bragan, before the 1947 season was half over, became one of Robinson's staunchest supporters and friends. On the other hand, Walker asked in writing to be traded. Several complications, however, prevented this until after the season had ended, and Walker, despite his reluctance, had to play through 1947 with Robinson on the team.

Rickey's action had prevented formal presentation of the petition. The rebellion had been quashed before it had gained enough momentum to become serious.

Now it was a week from opening day. Everyone was clamoring for Robinson to be promoted to the Dodgers. Hopper, the Montreal manager, complained to Rickey that Robinson's presence at first base was making it impossible for his regular first baseman to get into proper shape.

Dodger pilot Durocher was fretting about his own first base situation. He was convinced that Robinson could play better than Howie Schultz or

Ed Stevens. In the Dodger-Montreal exhibition series in Panama, Jackie had batted .625 and stolen seven bases. While still not perfect in covering the strange first base position, he was good enough to get by and was improving daily.

On April 9th, Montreal and the Dodgers returned to Brooklyn for two exhibition games before each team would go its separate ways. Robinson was still in the Montreal line-up and beginning to grow uneasy. With opening day so close, when was Rickey going to make up his mind?

As it turned out, Rickey's mind, in effect, was made up for him. It rained on April 9th, and the Montreal-Dodger game was called. Rickey and the Dodger front office staff, including Manager Leo Durocher, repaired to the executive offices on Montague Street to formulate plans for the season.

The opening day's line-up was discussed. Robinson's name was brought up.

"How about it, B.R.?" Durocher inquired. "We getting Robinson to play first—or not?"

Rickey blinked innocently. "You want him?"

"Of course I want him," Durocher said. "I need him. He can do us more good in the line-up than Schultz or Stevens. He murdered us in Panama."

"How about the rest of the men? You think they want him?"

Durocher hesitated. "Let's say they're not dead against him. They may not welcome Robinson with open arms, but they'll accept him. And once they see him playing good ball, they'll forget what color he is."

Rickey beamed. "Well, in that case—" The urgent ring of the telephone cut him short. He lifted the receiver, listened a moment, frowned. "Very well," he said, then hung up.

When Rickey turned back to the Dodger staff, his face was pale. He fumbled in the breast pocket of his jacket for a cigar. His fingers shook as he removed the cellophane wrapper.

The others waited silently. Something was up. They could sense it.

Finally Rickey spoke, his voice hoarse and strained.

"Harold," he nodded to Dodger traveling secretary Harold Parrott, "Commissioner Chandler has fined you five hundred dollars for writing and talking."

Parrott jerked upright in his chair. He opened his mouth to protest but Rickey held up his hand for silence.

"The commissioner has fined me, too. And the New York Yankees. Fined us two thousand dollars."

The others waited for him to go on. There was something in his voice that hinted the worst was yet to come.

Rickey drummed his fingers on the desk. Then

he turned his chair around to face Manager Durocher. "Leo," he said quietly, "the commissioner has suspended you from baseball for one year."

The statement hit the room like a bomb. Everyone was stunned into silence. Then Durocher, half numb from shock, stammered, "A—a year! But what for?"

"For conduct detrimental to baseball."

The foregoing was the climax to a series of run-ins Durocher had been having with the baseball commissioner, largely due to what Chandler called Leo's "questionable associations" off the playing field. The latest incident had occurred in Havana, when Durocher had brought to the commissioner's attention the presence of notorious gamblers near the Yankee dugout during a Dodger-Yankee exhibition game.

Durocher complained to Commissioner Chandler that had he been the one seen near the gamblers, he'd have been severely reprimanded for it, while no one had said anything to the Yankees.

A public squabble resulted among Chandler, Durocher, Rickey and Yankee president Larry Mac-Phail. Parrott, who was then writing a column for the Brooklyn *Eagle,* voiced his opinion in that space, which accounted for his being fined later.

By the time the Dodgers had returned to Brooklyn, the matter appeared to have been settled without any action from Chandler's office.

Then, seemingly out of nowhere came the commissioner's blow that morning of April 9th.

The suspension of Durocher spiked Rickey's plan to have the Dodger manager ask for the promotion of Robinson. At the same time, Rickey saw in the hue and cry about Durocher being raised in the press a perfect cover. Some of the furor attending the signing of Robinson would be mitigated by the Durocher story, and at the same time the excitement of it would give a lift to the depressed ball club, the fans and the front office.

Early the next morning, Rickey summoned Jackie to his office and summarily signed him to a Brooklyn Dodger contract calling for five thousand dollars for the season.

"Don't say anything yet, Jackie," Rickey told the ballplayer. "I want the announcement to come from here. I'll make it sometime during the afternoon."

With the knowledge burning within him that he was now a Dodger, the first Negro to play in the major leagues, Jackie took the field several hours later in a Montreal uniform. He tried to keep the tremendous tide of excitement rising in his body from showing itself on his face, or in his actions.

In the fifth inning, with a Montreal player on first base, Robinson strode to the plate. Coaching at third base, Manager Clay Hopper flashed the bunt sign. Jackie stepped in and waited for the first pitch.

At that exact moment, Branch Rickey's assistant Arthur Mann was walking slowly along the press box, depositing a sheet of paper in front of each sports writer.

Jackie bunted on the first pitch, but too sharply. The pitcher grabbed the ground ball, spun and threw to second for the first out. The throw went back to first to nip Jackie for the double play. As Jackie turned and trotted back to the dugout, he saw that the Montreal players were standing up off the bench, shouting and waving at him. In the third base coaching box Manager Hopper was waving his arms, a wide grin on his face.

Up in the press box, the tumult approached pandemonium as the sports writers leaped for the phones and the telegraphers began tapping out over their keys the historic news. In front of them was a simple sheet of paper presented by Arthur Mann. On the paper was one neatly typed sentence.

"The Brooklyn Dodgers today purchased the contract of Jackie Robinson from Montreal."

CHAPTER THIRTEEN

THE Brooklyn Dodgers of 1947 were favored to win the pennant, even without Leo Durocher at the helm. Their pitching staff looked good, and it was deep. There were Ralph Branca, Hank Behrman, Vic Lombardi, Rex Barney, Harry Taylor, Joe Hatten, and in the bullpen Hugh Casey.

Catching was Bruce Edwards. In the outfield the Dodgers had Dixie Walker, Pete Reiser and Gene Hermanski rotating with Carl Furillo. The infield had Johnny Jorgensen and Cookie Lavagetto sharing third base duties, Pee Wee Reese at shortstop, Eddie Stanky at second and Jackie Robinson at first. In the batting order, Robinson, an excellent bunter, hit second behind lead-off man Eddie Stanky.

Opening day was at Ebbets Field, the Dodgers against the Braves. The Brooklyn ball park was jammed to the rafters. Once again Robinson was on exhibition. The fans were restless, excited, expectant. Playing for Montreal was one thing; playing for the Dodgers was something else again.

Would Jackie make it, or would he prove unequal to the test of major league competiton? The fans were there to judge, to see how the enemy players reacted to Jackie and, indeed, to see how his own teammates acted in the heat of competition.

Considering how much was expected, the fans went home disappointed. True, the Dodgers won, 5–3. But they saw nothing to inspire enthusiasm about Robinson.

In the first inning he grounded to the third baseman. Then he flied out, hit into a double play, was safe on an error and finally was removed in the ninth inning for defensive purposes.

There was nothing to be seen, either, in the matter of friction between Jackie and the players. Both on the field and on the bench he was quiet. His teammates neither avoided him nor went out of their way to talk to him. The Boston players rode him from the bench mildly without any reference to his color.

The Dodgers won an uneventful next game, too. Jackie got his first hit, a bunt single.

The next day, when they moved to the Polo Grounds for a series with the Giants, the Dodgers were joined by their new manager Burt Shotton.

Rickey had brought the sixty-three-year-old, mild-appearing Shotton out of semiretirement to manage the Brooklyn Club.

The Dodgers greeted their new skipper with a 10–4 victory over their traditional rivals, Robinson contributing a single and his first major league home run to the attack.

The Dodgers were off and running, and so far there had been no incidents. Robinson's playing was below his normal capabilities, but this was attributed to the initial pressure.

Then the Philadelphia Phillies, managed by Ben Chapman, came to Ebbets Field—and it started.

Jackie came to bat in the first inning. As he walked slowly, with that pigeon-toed gait of his, toward home plate, the Philadelphia dugout erupted in a shower of racial insults. Manager Chapman led the tirade.

"Hey, nigger! Why don't you go back where you came from?"

"They're waiting for you in the jungles, black boy. Why don't you go back there?"

"We don't want you here, nigger!"

"Go back to the bushes, black boy!"

Jackie bit his lips. Well, the boss said I'd be getting the works, he thought grimly. I guess this is it.

As the game progressed, the abuse increased in virulence. The Dodger players were beginning to stir at the viciousness of the Philadelphia attack on Robinson. Inning after inning they saw Jackie take it without a murmur.

A Dodger player finally broke the ice midway through the game. There was a left-handed-hitting Philadelphia batter up at the plate. Eddie Stanky, the scrappy Dodger second baseman, called time and trotted over toward first, motioning Robinson to meet him.

"This guy likes to pull the inside pitch down the line," Stanky cautioned the first baseman. "It's a good idea to play him a little closer than usual toward the bag."

Jackie nodded his thanks and started to turn away. As he did, Stanky patted him on the back with his glove. "Don't let those bums get you down," he said. Robinson trotted back to his fielding position. He felt the load lift from his shoulders, just slightly.

Through seven innings, the Dodgers' Hal Gregg and Dutch Leonard, Philadelphia's knuckle ball expert, were locked in a scoreless duel. Gregg got the Phillies out in the eighth. Then the Dodgers came to bat.

Robinson led off. The racial epithets began at once from the direction of the visiting bench. Behind him, as he left the Dodger dugout, Jackie heard several of the Dodgers growling about the Philadelphians' lack of fair play.

Grimly, Jackie strode to the plate. He let Leonard's first pitch go by for a ball, then rapped the next pitch into center field for a single.

Gene Hermanski came up to hit and Robinson took his lead off first. He hadn't stolen a base yet in the major leagues. His anger was cold now. He watched carefully as Leonard worked. He knew the knuckle ball was an erratic pitch, difficult for the catcher to handle.

On the third pitch, Robinson took off for second base. The crowd leaped to its feet. This was the Robinson they had heard and read about!

Jackie had gotten a good jump. The pitch came in low to catcher Andy Seminick. He grabbed it and threw to second, but Jackie was in safely. The ball, thrown hurriedly by Seminick, bounced into the dirt, past the shortstop covering the base, and into center field. Jackie scrambled to his feet and sped into third standing up. The crowd gave him an ovation.

Then Hermanski singled, Jackie trotted home— and that was the game. Gregg set the Phillies down in the ninth for a 1–0 Dodger victory. Robinson had answered Philadelphia the way he was to answer during the next ten years all those in baseball who would victimize him because of his color—by knocking their brains out on the playing field.

It didn't always work out that way. The Dodgers swung out on their first western trip and plunged into disaster. While Robinson continued to be abused in the western cities with attacks less vitriolic than those suffered from Philadelphia, but certainly more coarse and personal than the average rookie is subjected to, the Dodgers were being abused by enemy batters and pitchers.

They won six and lost eleven on that swing through the West, and when they returned to Ebbets Field, they were in fifth place in the standings.

Early in May, there was instigated a new conspiracy to drive Robinson out of baseball. A member of the Dodgers, one of those originally opposed to Jackie, contacted members of the St. Louis Cardinals, the majority of whom were also opposed to Robinson. Plans were formulated for a strike by the St. Louis players on the occasion of their first invasion of Ebbets Field on May 6th.

According to the plan, the Cardinals were to refuse to take the field if the Dodgers insisted on playing Robinson. The Dodger player behind the conspiracy, for his part, was to announce his sympathy with the Cardinal players, then recruit as many other Dodgers into the strike plan as he could.

The strike did not come off on May 6th. Instead, the Cardinals and the rebellious Dodger player conceived the idea of making it a league-wide protest. But they had waited too long.

Somehow, knowledge of the plan had leaked to the then sports editor of the New York *Herald*

Tribune, Stanley Woodward, a man with a long-standing record as a defender of human rights, in or out of sports.

Woodward's instincts for a scoop and for justice rose equally to the occasion. He sniffed around quietly. He knew that Sam Breadon, president of the St. Louis Club, was in New York at the moment, ostensibly to confer with manager Eddie Dyer about the Cardinals' poor playing.

"The Coach," as Woodward was affectionately called by fellow sports writers, knew, too, that Ford Frick, the National League president, was in town. Something was up, all right.

Woodward sat down at his typewriter and pounded out the story. Then he confronted Frick and Breadon with the article before it was scheduled to go to press. The two men had no choice but to confirm Woodward's scoop—but off the record.

"If you print the story," they told Woodward, "we will neither deny nor admit the truth of your statements."

"That's good enough," the sports editor declared. "A 'No comment' from either of you will be enough confirmation of my story."

On the morning of May 9th, Stanley Woodward, armed with additional information gained from Breadon, Frick and the player who had originally tipped him to the plan, broke the story in the *Herald Tribune.*

"The strike has been temporarily averted and perhaps permanently quashed," Woodward said, after a series of conferences among the St. Louis players, Breadon and Frick.

"The commissioner," added Woodward, "has taken a firm stand against the Cardinal players."

"If you do this," Frick said to the Cardinals, "you will be suspended from the league. You will find that the friends you think you have in the press box will not support you, that you will be outcasts. I don't care if half the league strikes. Those who do it will encounter quick retribution. All will be suspended and I don't care if it wrecks the National League for five years. This is the United States of America and one citizen has as much right to play as another.

"The National League will go down the line with Robinson, whatever the consequences. You will find if you go through with your intention that you have been guilty of complete madness."

Frick's forthright stand cut the legs from under the conspiracy. Meanwhile, the rest of the newspapers jumped on the story. Frick recanted his original statement to Woodward that he would not comment, and admitted to reporters that there had been some meetings between himself and Breadon, but he minimized the strike threat as being simply a stir of dissatisfaction among some of the Cardinals.

Football hero at UCLA

Wide World Photos
Branch Rickey looking on as Jackie Robinson signs
his 1948 Brooklyn Dodgers' contract

The glory days with the Brooklyn
Dodgers: hitting a home run;
a bang-bang double play;
stealing home

The heart of
the Dodgers
batting order:
Duke Snider;
Gil Hodges;
Jackie Robinson;
PeeWee Reese;
Roy Campanella

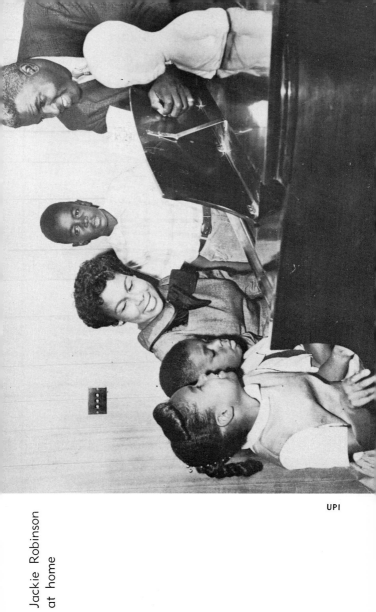

Jackie Robinson
at home

The end of a brilliant baseball career

Jackie receives Doctor of Laws degree at
Howard University (Reverend Martin Luther
King in rear)

As Jackie looked a few years ago when he was
elected to the baseball Hall of Fame

UPI

Breadon and the St. Louis manager Eddie Dyer, however, branded the story as "ridiculous."

Hard on the heels of this pressure came a new threat, this one apparently more serious and physical. The day after the St. Louis strike threat hit the newspapers, it was revealed that the Dodger offices and Jackie himself had received notes in the mail threatening to kill the Negro player if he didn't "get out of baseball."

Although the unsigned letters were regarded as the work of a crank, they still made Jackie nervous. And the same day, when the Dodgers moved into Philadelphia for a series with the Phillies, the Benjamin Franklin Hotel barred Jackie from rooming with his teammates. (St. Louis was the only other city in the league which forced Robinson into separate accommodations.)

The pressure of the past two days' events had by now worn Jackie's nerves to the shattering point. The St. Louis Cardinals' strike threat, the warning that he would be shot if he showed up again on a ball field, the hotel's edict against him—all had come within the last forty-eight hours.

And all Jackie could do was to keep his mouth shut and take it. That was all he could do, at least, if he wanted to remain in organized baseball. Rickey had warned him that if he lost his temper, if he complained or popped off at the treatment he was getting, the anti-Negro element would leap in immediately to brand him a "troublemaker."

No, all he could do when the reporters gathered around him in Philadelphia's Shibe Park was grin and talk pleasantly, though the blood pounded in his temples and his chest was bursting with pent-up anger.

"I'm just going ahead, playing the best ball I know how and doing my best to make good," was what he said to the sports writers. He did add, however, "Brother, it's rugged."

Rugged was the word, especially in Philadelphia. The Phillies now had added ammunition to throw at Jackie. They augmented their usual racial assault with allusion to the shooting threat against Robinson. In the dugout, the players held their bats as though they were machine guns, pointed them at Jackie and made appropriate shooting noises.

Some of the home fans behind the Philadelphia dugout joined in the "fun." One in particular got on Robinson especially hard. And the effect on one of the Dodgers was somewhat startling.

Pee Wee Reese, the veteran Dodger shortstop from Kentucky, called for time and trotted over to Jackie's position. He began talking to Robinson about the Philadelphia hitters due up that inning, using that excuse to drape his arm in friendly fashion around Jackie's shoulders.

It was a tremendous gesture of support from one of the most-respected and best-liked players in baseball—and one with a southern background at that. Later, questioned by sports writers about his feelings on Jackie, Reese gave a unique reply, one which had significant effect on many a player's attitude toward Robinson.

"When I first met Robinson in spring training," Reese said, "I figured, well, let me give this guy a chance. It may be he's just as good as I am. Lately I've changed my mind. Now I think maybe he's better than I am. Frankly, I don't think I'd stand up under the kind of thing he's been subjected to as well as he's taking it."

National League president Ford Frick again stepped into the picture. He warned Ben Chapman, the Philadelphia manager, to keep his bench jockeying of Robinson free from racial slurs.

"I don't expect Philadelphia, or any other team, to handle Jackie Robinson with kid gloves," Frick told Chapman. "But let's keep the blows above the belt."

Despite the moral support, Jackie's play fell off. He was worried about the seemingly concerted pressure against him around the league. In addition, he was still unsure of himself around first base. There were plays he looked awkward at making, and on one occasion a Dodger pitcher blew up at him after he'd made an error that nearly cost the hurler the ball game.

He went into a desperate batting slump. Twenty-one times he went to the plate and got only one hit for his efforts. During that period he actually reached base more times by the ball hitting him than by him hitting the ball. Six times during the opening weeks of the season Robinson was hit by the pitch, a rather unique, though reluctantly held, record.

There was talk of benching Robinson in favor of Schultz, but neither Rickey nor Manager Shotton would hear of it. "Just wait," Rickey told the sports writers. "Robinson has been under terrible pressure. Wait until he loosens up."

Jackie's average plummeted to .230. Then the Phillies moved once again to Ebbets Field. Because of their attacks against him, Jackie made it a point to try a little extra hard against them, and in the third game of the series, he broke loose at last.

Going into the fourth inning of that game, the Phillies held a 2–0 lead. The Dodgers hadn't been able to touch Philadelphia hurler Dick Mauney. Then Jackie, leading off in the fourth, cracked Mauney's first pitch for a single to left field. That opened the gates. Four straight hits followed, and before Manger Chapman could pull his pitcher out, the Dodgers had scored three times to take the lead.

In the sixth inning, with one out, Reese walked. As Robinson stepped up to hit, he got the hit-and-run sign from the third base coach. Jackie promptly rapped relief pitcher Tommy Hughes's first pitch to right center field and Reese, running with the pitch, easily made third.

Then Jackie began to dance off first base, threatening to steal, challenging the pitcher to a duel of nerves. Twice Hughes threw back to first, but Jackie was there ahead of the throw, grinning at the man on the mound. Again Robinson led off, bluffed a run at second. Reese at the same time bluffed a run off third base. Hughes, flustered, started to pitch to the plate, stopped, turned—and balked.

Reese trotted across the plate with the Dodgers' fourth run and Robinson advanced to second. The Ebbets Field crowd loved it, and they let Robinson know with their cheers.

In the eighth inning the Phillies crept closer, adding a run to make the score 4–3. But this was Robinson's day to shake loose. With two out and nobody on base, he walloped a home run deep into the left field seats, his second homer of the season. That cushioned the lead for Dodger hurler Joe Hatten, 5–3, and that was the final score.

The victory moved the Dodgers into third place in the league, one game behind the league-leading New York Giants. In the Dodger clubhouse after the game, some of the Dodger players came around to shake hands with Jackie.

"Nice going, Jackie."

"Atta boy, Jack."

"That's hitting them where it hurts, Jackie."

Manager Shotton was smiling. "Maybe this is the turn of the tide," he said.

Robinson and the Dodgers began to move upward. In the middle of June Jackie started a hitting streak that reached twenty-one games, just one short of the rookie record established by Johnny Mize more than ten years earlier. His fielding was becoming more assured, his base running more aggressive.

There was a night game at Pittsburgh on June 24th. In the fifth inning, with the scored tied at 2–2, Robinson singled with two out and went to third on a single by Hermanski. He stepped off third quietly and watched as Pittsburgh pitcher Fritz Ostermueller wound up to pich to the next batter. Ostermueller hardly glanced Jackie's way. The pitch was a ball.

Jackie eased open his lead off third. Then, when Ostermueller started his windup, Robinson took off for the plate. The crowd roared. The catcher frantically waved to Ostermueller to throw the ball. Jackie thundered down the line as the fans yelled in appreciation of one of baseball's most exciting feats. The catcher squatted to block off the plate.

The ball came in, Jackie slid across in a cloud of dust—and was safe!

Several of the Dodgers leaped off the bench to greet Jackie as he trotted over, pounding the dirt out of his uniform. The thrilling steal of home—Jackie's first, but far from the last in the major leagues—put the Dodgers in front, 3–2. It proved to be the winning run, too, though the Dodgers added an extra tally in the eighth inning to make the final score 4–2.

Branch Rickey, sitting in a box seat behind the Dodger dugout, was beaming from ear to ear. "But wait," he predicted. "They haven't seen Robinson in action on the bases yet—not really. They may not see him at his best this year at all, or even next year. He's still in his shell. When he comes out for good, he'll have them comparing him with Cobb."

On the impetus of Robinson's twenty-one-game hitting streak, the Dodgers moved into first place in July. Jackie's position on the Dodgers was now permanent. Rickey sold Schultz to the Phillies and Eddie Stevens was optioned to Montreal.

The Dodger president thus let the rest of the baseball world know: Come what may, Jackie Robinson was the Brooklyn Dodgers' first baseman.

In many quarters, the inevitable was not accepted graciously. The St. Louis Cardinals were still smarting from the embarrassment of their aborted strike against Jackie. Their hostility was by no means unanimous, but the anti-Robinson element on the club was in the majority.

The Cardinals came to Brooklyn in the latter part of August hot on the league-leading Dodgers' trail. Brooklyn took the first two games. the Cardinals won the third. The fourth game, played in a World Series' atmosphere of tension, went into extra innings, tied 2–2.

In the eleventh inning, the Cardinals had Stan Musial on first base with one out. Enos Slaughter, the St. Louis outfielder, was at bat. On the one-and-one pitch, Slaughter hit a sharp grounder to Robinson. Jackie wheeled to see whether he had a play on Musial at second, saw he hadn't and raced to first base ahead of Slaughter.

Jackie had already touched first and turned to keep Musial anchored at second base when Slaughter reached him. As the Cardinal player crossed the bag, his left foot came down heavily on Jackie's ankle. Robinson yelled and limped away, blood streaming from his foot.

Dodger trainer Doc Wendler raced out from the dugout. Eddie Stanky ran over from second base, Reese from shortstop. Robinson was sitting on the ground, holding his injured foot.

"I'm okay," he said to Wendler. "Stick a quick bandage on it and I'll be okay. It's just a little gash."

The trainer probed the wound expertly. "Some little gash," he snorted. He motioned to the Dodgers on the bench. "Couple of you guys help me carry him downstairs," he said.

"Carry me!" Jackie exploded. He stood up painfully. He tried to walk but the agony grabbed at him. "Just let me lean on you, Doc," he pleaded to Wendler. "I want to walk off the field."

The Dodgers lost the game in the next inning, but in the clubhouse later, the players talked angrily of Jackie's spiking rather than their loss. Dodger secretary Harold Parrott stormed into the room.

"I told them off, every last one of them. What a dirty trick! I told them to their faces that it was deliberate, and I told them what would happen if they ever tried anything like that again."

Doc Wendler, treating Jackie's ankle and calf for cuts and contusions, shook his head grimly.

"Jackie was lucky he wasn't maimed. I can't understand how one ballplayer could deliberately do that to another. He might have severed Jackie's Achilles' tendon and finished his baseball career."

Again, Robinson answered back in kind—his kind. On the final western swing of the year, with the pennant in the balance, Jackie played spectacular ball. In game after game he paced the Dodger attack. Then came the crucial final series with St.

131

Louis. Three games to be played, and the Dodgers knew they had to take at least two out of the three to check the last-ditch surge of the Red Birds.

Jackie saw to that, practically by himself. In the three games he raked Cardinal hurlers for a home run, a double and four singles in thirteen times at bat—a .462 average. The Dodgers won their two out of three, leaving behind them a beaten foe.

Except for the mathematical finality, the Dodgers had clinched the pennant. They had won seven out of ten games in the West and beaten off the last charge of the runner-up Cardinals. In those ten games Robinson had hit at a .400 pace to lift his batting average to .301. In his sixteen hits over that span were included three home runs and three doubles.

Several days later, on September 12th, Jackie was named "Rookie of the Year" by the St. Louis *Sporting News,* the baseball "Bible." Editor J. G. Taylor Spink, in announcing the award, commented, "Robinson was rated and examined solely as a freshman player in the big leagues—on the basis of his hitting, his running, his defensive play, his team value.

"The sociological experiment that Robinson represented, the trail blazing that he did, the barriers he broke down, did not enter into the decisions."

The Jackie Robinson bandwagon had been

launched. A week later, the Dodgers returned to Brooklyn from games at Philadelphia and Pittsburgh. The pennant was theirs now, the first one to fly over Brooklyn since 1941. More than three thousand wildly cheering fans met the Dodger train at New York's Pennsylvania Station.

As the "General" slid into the station from Pittsburgh, the zany Ebbets Field "Symphoney" band struck up "Hail, Hail, the Gang's All Here." Squads of special police strained and tugged to keep the crowd in place as the Dodger players stepped off the train.

"There's Dixie!" They screamed. And "Pee Wee!" "Jackie!"

Shrieking fans burst through the police barrier. They grabbed at Dixie Walker, tearing at his clothes for souvenirs. They grabbed Reese, catcher Bruce Edwards, pitcher Ralph Branca. But they really mobbed Jackie Robinson.

White and Negro, they pawed at Jackie for autographs, pummeled him on the back and shook his hand till it was limp and cramped. Jackie broke away momentarily and charged into a phone booth to call his wife. The crowd chased him, pressed against the booth so tightly he couldn't get out.

Six policemen broke a path through the mob to rescue Jackie. They escorted him to the subway, followed by hundreds of howling fans. Robinson fled through a turnstile as a train pulled into the station. Scores of fans followed him, leaping over and crawling under the stiles to get into the same train.

It was a great ride back to Brooklyn.

On September 23rd, the citizens of Brooklyn declared a "Jackie Robinson Day." In pregame ceremonies at Ebbets Field, Jackie was given a Cadillac sedan, a gold watch, assorted gifts ranging from television sets to an electric broiler, and various testimonial speeches.

Perhaps the most fitting tribute to Jackie, however, was the appearance in a relief role during the game of pitcher Dan Bankhead. The hurler had been bought by Rickey a month earlier to bolster the Dodger pitching staff for the tough days of the waning pennant race.

His entry into the game drew scarcely a ripple of interest from the huge Ebbets Field crowd.

Yet pitcher Dan Bankhead was a Negro.

CHAPTER FOURTEEN

A strictly underdog Dodger team earned the honor of carrying the powerful New York Yankees to seven games in the 1947 World Series. The Bronx Bombers had Joe DiMaggio, Tommy Henrich, Yogi Berra, Johnny Lindell, Phil Rizzuto and George McQuinn in their batting order. Their pitching was awesome, with Allie Reynolds, Frank Shea, Vic Raschi, Floyd Bevens, Bobo Newson, Carl Drews and the relief pitching sensation Joe Page.

Jackie Robinson, the first Negro to play in a World Series game, also became the 1947 series' first base runner. While his wife Rae, and his mother, who had come east for the World Series, watched anxiously from the stands, Jackie worked Yankee pitcher Frank Shea for a walk with one out in the first inning.

On the first pitch to Pete Reiser Jackie stole second on rookie catcher Yogi Berra. Then Reiser hit a ground ball to first. Jackie headed for third, but first baseman McQuinn threw to third and cut him off. Jackie stopped short midway between second and third.

Back and forth between the bases he jockeyed in the rundown. He knew he was a dead duck, but he was trying to keep alive long enough to enable Reiser to run all the way to second. At this tactic, Jackie was a master. His football experience had taught him to run in quick starts and stops. And while the Yankee Stadium echoed with the appreciation of his base running wizardry, Jackie kept the Yankees at bay until Reiser, indeed, made it all the way to second.

Robinson's effort promptly paid off as Walker singled to score Reiser for a 1–0 Dodger lead.

The run looked big until the fifth. Then the roof fell in on Ralph Branca. Five Yankee runs poured across the plate. DiMaggio singled, McQuinn walked, Johnson was hit by the pitch. Lindell doubled for two runs and Rizzuto walked, reloading the bases.

Then Branca walked—to the showers. He pitched two straight balls to pinch hitter Bobby Brown and was replaced by Hank Behrman. The relief pitcher walked Brown to force in the third run. Stirnweiss hit into a force play at the plate, but Henrich singled for the final two runs of the inning.

In the sixth inning Jackie walked again. Then he danced off first until he forced Shea into a balk. From second he scored on a pinch-hit single by Carl Furillo. But it was the Yankees' ball game, 5–3.

The second game was a contest for four innings, then the Yankees broke it open and ran off with an easy 10–3 victory. Robinson contributed a double and a single and batted in a run for his losing cause.

Yankee fans were predicting another patented Yankee sweep of the series, but the Dodgers stormed back to outslug the Bombers 9–8 in Ebbets Field. Robinson singled twice and stole his second base of the series.

The fourth game is a World Series classic, one of the most dramatic in baseball history. Floyd Bevens went into the ninth inning of that game pitching a no-hitter against Brooklyn. His wildness, however, had yielded a run in the fifth on two walks, a sacrifice and an infield out, but he was leading, 2–1.

With one out in the ninth, Bevens walked Furillo. Jorgensen fouled out. Bevens was one out away from a no-hitter now. Manager Shotton sent in the speedy Al Gionfriddo to run for Furillo, and Reiser up to pinch-hit for pitcher Hugh Casey.

Gionfriddo promptly stole second on Berra, who was having a miserable series behind the plate.

Yankee manager Bucky Harris ordered the long-ball-hitting Reiser intentionally passed, violating the baseball stratagem that forbids putting the potentially winning run on base deliberately.

Shotton countered by sending Lavagetto up to hit for Stanky, and Miksis in to run for Resier. And the game of chess went to Shotton as Lavagetto, in one blow, wrecked Bevens' no-hitter, beat the Yankees and tied the series. On Bevens' second pitch, Cookie rapped a double off the right field wall and both runners scored, for a 3–2 Dodger victory.

The Yankees were shaken, but Shea brought them back with a 2–1 decision in the next game. Robinson drove in the lone Dodger run in the sixth inning, singling Gionfriddo home from second.

Still the Dodgers wouldn't say die. They tied the series once more, winning the sixth game, 8–6. Robinson rapped a double and a single, scored one run and batted one in. But that was all for Jackie and the Dodgers.

Shea, Bevens and Page combined in the seventh game to hold Robinson hitless and the Dodgers to two runs. The Yankees won the game, 5–2, and locked up another in a long string of World Championships.

Without being spectacular, it hadn't been a bad World Series for Robinson. He got seven hits, for a .259 average, batted in three runs, scored three

138

and stole two bases. He also handled fifty-five chances at first base without an error.

In the Dodger dressing room after the final game, the players showered, dressed quietly and left the ball park. The long season was over. They had acquitted themselves creditably against the Yankees, even if they didn't win. There were friendly cries of "So long" and "See you in spring training" and "Have a good winter."

Robinson sat on the stool in front of his locker and dressed slowly, thinking of the many things that had happened to him during that hectic season. All the insults had been there, as Rickey had warned him. He recalled bitterly for the moment the taunting of the Phillies, the strike threats. He looked down at his bare left foot. The ankle area was still marked with the spike wounds given to him by Enos Slaughter.

But there were the good things, too. Except for very few of the Dodgers, he had been accepted on the Brooklyn club. He hit a solid .297 in helping them win the pennant. He led the league in stolen bases with twenty-nine, hit twelve home runs, scored one hundred and twenty-five times and drove across forty-eight runs.

Yes, the Dodgers had accepted him—but not as "one of the boys," he knew. Perhaps he would never be that. For the most part, he had not been included in the usual clubhouse horseplay, in the "bull" sessions and card games on the road. But once Bruce Edwards and Pee Wee Reese had asked him to join them in a round of golf. Many of the Dodgers, in the interest of teamwork and fair play, if nothing else, had gone out of their way to point things out to him, little things that helped his game.

Jackie laced on his shoes and stood up to leave. He had taken the worst they could hand out, he felt. Perhaps next year would be somewhat easier. He grinned to himself ruefully. If it got any harder, he'd either crack up or take a baseball bat to somebody's skull.

Robinson picked up his suitcase and went out into the autumn air—and his first round on the "banquet circuit." Ballplayers, if they are anything special at all, spend many of their off-season nights making public appearances at dinners, lodge meetings, youth organizations, theaters, radio and TV shows and what have you.

And Robinson was something very special. A nationwide theater tour, testimonial dinners in his honor, a Hollywood movie of his life was being planned.

It was a chance for Jackie to make a good deal of extra money, and Branch Rickey was happy enough to let him make it. Besides, he wanted

Jackie to go out and meet the world as any other Dodger player would.

And Jackie was, indeed, wined and dined. In Chicago the local chapter of the Baseball Writers Association named him their "Rookie of the Year." In Los Angeles a UCLA alumni club honored him with a luncheon. Round and round the banquet circuit Jackie traveled. In December Hollywood started "The Jackie Robinson Story," starring Jackie Robinson, Ruby Dee, and featuring Branch Rickey.

At a dinner in Washington, Robinson for the first time opened his mouth and put his foot in it. With the local sports writers present, Jackie stated, mildly but unequivocally, that he was disappointed at not receiving a raise during the 1947 season, though he apparently deserved one by being named "Rookie of the Year."

Robinson was not in the least bit rancorous. But it hadn't occurred to him that with many members of the sports writing fraternity, Rickey was unaffectionately known as "El Cheapo." These writers therefore indulged their favorite columnar sport— roasting Rickey over their typewriter coals, while the rest of the fraternity berated Robinson for "popping off"—an expression that would become increasingly synonymous with any public statement made by Jackie down through the years.

There was no question about Robinson getting a raise for the 1948 season. On February 12th

Branch Rickey called a press conference at his Montague Street offices in Brooklyn to announce the signing of Robinson and pitcher Hugh Casey.

For any number of reasons, exact salary figures are never revealed by the ball clubs. But it was estimated that Jackie's 1948 contract called for close to fifteen thousand dollars, almost three times his rookie salary.

The sports writers asked Jackie the usual questions. How was he feeling, was he keeping in shape, did he think he might win the batting championship next season? Then one of the writers asked, "Would you like to try out for second base this time, Jackie?"

Robinson's tongue was still burning from his Washington statement. This time he would measure his words. "I don't see how anyone on our ball club can push Stanky off," he said. "He's a heck of a second baseman. Of course, I feel that I might be better at another position, but if they want me to play first, it's all right with me."

A diplomatic statement by Jackie. But Rickey had made up his own mind even before the 1947 season had ended. And during the World Series he had remarked with deliberate casualness to a reporter:

"The best second baseman in the world is playing first base."

CHAPTER FIFTEEN

IT is quite probable that the adulation that he was accorded over the winter months did not go completely to Jackie Robinson's head. On the other hand, there is no doubt that it would have been far better were it, indeed, Jackie's head that had swollen to outlandish proportions. Instead it was his waistline. The chicken dinners and lack of exercise had taken their toll. From the hard 195-pounder who had reported to the Dodgers the year before, Robinson had ballooned to a fat 220 pounds.

There was no hiding it. When Jackie reported to the Dodgers at their Dominican Republic training camp, the shock was heard all the way back to Brooklyn. The writers who were traveling with the club immediately wired back the news.

"Robinson is hog fat!"

Jackie's condition was the big issue of the training season, and with good reason. Rickey had committed himself to a deal which would shortly be sending Eddie Stanky off to the Boston Braves. If Robinson floundered, the Dodgers would be required to play Eddie Miksis at second. Miksis could field superbly, but he couldn't hit. And then, who would play first?

Leo Durocher, rehired by Rickey after his year's suspension, was not a manager to mince words. He might have avoided a good deal of friction had he gone to Robinson directly and bawled him out, but "popping off" in front of newspapermen was a Durocher specialty long before Robison donned his first pair of long pants.

"One year in the big leagues and he's a hero!" the acidulous Leo stormed. "Who does he think he is, reporting for training looking like a sausage? Does he think he's got a guarantee I can't stick him on the bench all year if I want to? Or trade him to some last-place club?"

To writers bored with the routine stories out of a baseball spring training camp, a star player nicking himself while shaving is news. Durocher's blast at Robinson, therefore, was a story worth cultivating and milking for all it was worth. The writers filed their stories to the New York newspapers and confronted Robinson, several days later, with the published reports.

Robinson's eyes blazed. "You fellows really did a job on me, didn't you!" he exclaimed. "Never mind giving me a chance to talk, to get some of the weight off. I know I came in overweight. But I've been working out, losing it gradually. The way you guys wrote it you'd think I was sitting around here all day drinking coconut milk!"

Jackie's explosion rocked the sports writers on their heels. They had expected a strong reaction from Robinson, but not that strong. It dawned on them at that moment that the humble-appearing Robinson of the year before had been under mighty strong wraps.

With the realization came renewed admiration for Jackie. "I don't know how a guy with a temper like Robinson's ever kept himself quiet last year when they were giving him the business," one of the writers remarked wonderingly.

"The guy must have been eating himself up alive all year, listening to those dirty cracks and not able to answer back," another agreed.

Some of the writers nevertheless took exception to Jackie's remarks. One wrote the next day that apparently Jackie had let his head swell during the winter, in addition to his midriff.

A heated three-way feud began to develop among Robinson, Durocher and several of the New York scribes. Though the passing of time and the mellowness of advancing age eventually cooled off all the parties concerned, there are undercurrents of this ill feeling which exist to the present day.

After all, Robinson's condition was a vital point. At twenty-nine, he was slow getting back into playing shape. Despite the urgency of the situation, everyone knew that to rush Jackie unduly would probably strain or severely injure his muscles and joints.

By nearly starving himself and working out under the tropical sun, he managed to drop fifteen pounds in two weeks. But he was still at least ten pounds over his best playing weight.

Neither the sports writers nor Manager Durocher let up on him. Every story that came out of the Dodger camp harped on Jackie's weight problem. The writers even tried to get Jackie on a scale, so they could see for themselves what he weighed.

This was not calculated to soothe Robinson's jagged nerves. Then Durocher jumped on him, again via an interview with the writers. Eddie Stanky had been traded to the Braves, and Leo wanted a perfectly conditioned man to take his place at second base. He wanted that man to be Jackie.

"Robinson is going to start playing second base for me right now," Durocher rasped. "Enough of this easy workout baloney. Who's kidding who with that baloney? He's still fat as a house and I am going to get on his back and stay there till that fat works off him!"

"But Leo," one writer put in, "Jackie claims he's

been losing weight right along. He says he's hustling like everybody else."

Durocher forced a derisive laugh. "Hustling? Listen, the only place you'll see Robinson hustling is to the dinner table. Hustling, my foot! Robinson is loafing! He isn't even trying to knock that weight down. But I'll do it for him!"

"Won't playing him at second in the exhibitions, before he's ready, do him more harm than good?" one writer wanted to know.

The Dodger manager snorted. "Listen, bending over for them ground balls is the only way Robinson's gonna get that blubber off his belly. If I had my way I'd have him climbing coconut trees all day. That'd slim him down fast."

But the weight was slow in coming off. In addition, Jackie developed a soreness in his arm. Durocher kept him at second base. He was determined to play Robinson into shape by opening day.

The Dodgers broke camp and moved back to the States for the start of their spring exhibition tour through the South. It was a history-making tour. For the first time in a number of southern cities, a Negro athlete was to be allowed to play against whites.

The Dodgers played in Dallas and Fort Worth in Texas; Oklahoma City, Oklahoma; Asheville, North Carolina; Newport News, Virginia; and in Baltimore, Maryland. The accomplishment of Robinson that spring toward breaking racial barriers throughout the South is immeasurable. What could be counted with precision, though, was the paid admissions to the ball games. Overflow crowds, swollen with the presence of Negroes who now had someone to root for, filled the parks in every city.

They found little for which to root, however. There was no denying the fact that Jackie's excess weight was slowing him down. His advertised speed afield and on the base paths was nowhere to be seen.

On opening day Robinson was still overweight. He wasn't running and he wasn't hitting. Neither were the rest of the Dodgers, which now included Negro catcher Roy Campanella. While Durocher fretted and fumed, Brooklyn floundered around the second divison.

The Brooklyn skipper was taking the Dodgers' failure as a personal insult. The year before, during his suspension, Shotton had come out of semiretirement to win the pennant. Now he, Leo, had been given a chance to make a comeback—only it was some comeback!

Under the daily pressure of playing, the fat began to melt from Robinson's frame. He started to hit again. In May he won two straight games with timely hits, one a tremendous home run with two on to beat Philadelphia.

In the field he began to feel comfortable once

more. Second base was more natural to him, and teamed with one of the best fielding shortstops in the majors in Pee Wee Reese, he had a new sense of security. In short order, he and Reese developed into a magnificent double-play combination.

In the latter part of the month the Dodgers amazed everyone in baseball when it was revealed that they'd asked for waivers on Robinson. Briefly, the waiver system operates like this:

Periodically, during the year, each of the major league teams circulates within its league a list of players, called a "waiver" list. The players on the list, theoretically, are up for sale at the "waiver" price of ten thousand dollars. To purchase a player, a team puts in a claim for him, first crack going to the team which is last in the standings. If that team passes on the player, the seventh-place team can claim him, and so on, in that reverse order of team standing.

If all teams pass on a particular player, the claim sequence continues in the other league. Finally, no claims having been entered on a player, he may be given his unconditional release.

The catch in the waiver system is that the list of players constitutes an offer that may be withdrawn at any time, with minor limitations, even after another team has indicated its intention to claim a player. In many cases the offering club has no intention of letting a player go to another team on waivers, even though his name be on the waiver list.

Why, then, is the name submitted? There may be several reasons, some of them buried in the mysterious workings of a club owner's mind. One of the most frequent uses of the waiver list is for bait.

For example, when a club puts forward a claim for a player, then the team waiving the man has a good idea that the claiming club is interested either in improving itself in general, or in that player in particular. In either case, the offering club has gained a valuable piece of knowledge. It can withdraw the player's name and offer him back to the interested club at a price higher than the standard waiver price, or it could perhaps swing an advantageous player trade armed with the knowledge that the other team is not completely happy with its present roster.

Jackie Robinson's name on the Dodgers' waiver list was quite probably bait, for the list was circulated well before the June 15th trading deadline. Moreover, the waiver lists are confidential, so that when Gus Steiger of the New York *Daily Mirror* reported his "scoop" on the morning of May 26th, it was less scoop than it was Branch Rickey guile.

The Dodger president was always a man seeking to kill two birds with one stone. While he had Jackie on the waiver list for bait, he waited for an opportune moment to "leak" the news, a moment when Robinson and the Dodgers might be in need of extra stimulus.

The time was now. Despite a recent upsurge in hitting by Robinson, the Dodgers continued to stagger. The revelation that Robinson's name was on a current waiver list might be just the thing to prod Jackie and the rest of the Dodgers into added hustle.

Any effect the news might have had on Jackie was nullified to a substantial extent by an injury to his left knee. In Cincinnati he collided with Ben Zientara of the Reds along the first base line. Zientara was knocked unconscious, and Jackie strained his knee tendons severely enough to be sidelined for several days.

It took more than a month for Jackie to regain his stride, and even after that he was periodically bothered by the effects of the injury. The Dodgers continued on their second division treadmill, with Manager Durocher growing more fretful and irascible.

Leo's position with the Dodgers was rapidly becoming untenable. He didn't want to resign, and Rickey didn't want to fire him. Yet something had to be done. In July, after a conference between Rickey and President Horace Stoneham of the New York Giants, it was announced that Burt Shotton was returning to manage the Dodgers, and that Durocher had become the manager of the Giants.

In New York City, this was considered tantamount to treason. For years Dodger fans had been schooled to hate the Giants with a single-mindedness exceeded only by the Giant fans' unremitting hatred of Leo Durocher.

Now partisans of both clubs were caught in the middle of their allegiances. Dodger adherents had to choose between loyalty to the man and loyalty to Brooklyn. Giant fans, in order to remain rooters of the team, were being asked to embrace the Devil himself.

Baseball players have no such problems. Some Dodgers regretted Durocher's loss, some Giants regretted his gain. It is doubtful that any player's performance was altered significantly by emotional upset. Robinson, understandably, was not sorry to see Leo go. He sincerely believed—and he said it often later—that Durocher was a great manager. But he and Leo reacted like two pieces of flint when in contact with each other.

At any rate, it just wasn't the Dodgers' year. Shotton brought them up to a third-place finish, behind Boston and St. Louis. If it was of any satisfaction to the Dodgers, Durocher could do no better than fifth with the Giants.

After his wretched start, Robinson closed out the season well. He batted .296, with twelve home runs and eighty-five runs batted in. He led the league in being hit by a pitched ball with seven, and in fielding average for second basemen with .983.

Jackie's most significant accomplishment that year is not mentioned in the record books, however.

It was during the night of August 24th, at Pittsburgh. For three innings the Dodger bench had been riding plate umpire Butch Henline. Then, in the fourth, Henline called a strike on Gene Hermanski, and the Dodger bench jockeys howled in pain. After Hermanski made out, the Dodgers continued their hooting.

Henline turned his head and yelled at the Dodger bench. "Get off my back, you guys. I'm just trying to umpire a ball game out here."

Robinson jeered back at the arbiter. "Yeah, well somebody certainly ought to!"

Henline wheeled and tore off his mask. His face beet red, he pointed his finger at Jackie.

"You! Robinson! Yer out of the game!"

Thrown out of his first ball game, Robinson was becoming one of the boys now. Certainly at that moment he was more so than ever before.

One of the New York papers headlined the story the next day: "Jackie Just Another Guy."

Well, that's what he had been trying to become in baseball—just another guy, playing the game like everybody else.

He was coming close—closer than he had thought possible in so short a period of time.

But Jackie had the secret knowledge that he would never make it all the way.

CHAPTER SIXTEEN

Jackie Robinson wasted no time informing the National League that things would be different in 1949. After a winter of working along with Roy Campanella at a Harlem Y.M.C.A., supervising sports activities of underprivileged youngsters, Jackie reported to the Dodgers at Vero Beach, Florida, trim and fit.

Gone was all excess flesh. Gone, too, was the last veil of obsequious manner Robinson had been forced to assume for two years. From the first day of spring training he was confident, volatile, aggressive.

"They'd better be rough on me this year," Jackie told a sports writer grimly. "Because I'm sure going to be rough on them."

Even in the intrasquad games at Vero Beach he played it that way. During one game the bench jockeying became particularly vicious on both sides.

In the last inning, with the verbal war still strong, Jackie came up to bat against a young farm hand named Chris Van Cuyk.

Robinson rapped the young hurler for a single. As he raced to first base, Jackie hollered out to the mound, "You'll be a Class D busher for twenty years."

The next time Robinson came up Van Cuyk sent him reeling back with a fast ball high inside. The pitcher came back again with a fast ball at the knees that forced Jackie to jump back from the plate. On the next pitch Robinson popped out.

"That's where your power is!" Van Cuyk jeered from the mound.

The game ended there and the players headed for the clubhouse. Robinson strode over to Van Cuyk.

"Listen, busher," Jackie snarled, "don't you throw at me again if you know what's good for you."

"Then you keep your mouth shut," Van Cuyk retorted.

"Talking is one thing, throwing at a man is another," Jackie said angrily. "Now I'm telling you—"

But before anything further could happen the Dodger players had separated the two men.

The altercation was soon forgotten, until Commissioner Happy Chandler, hearing of the incident and Robinson's statement—"I'm going to be rough on them this year"—brought the affair back into focus. He called Robinson to Miami and gave him a dressing down.

"Baseball doesn't tolerate fighting of any kind," Chandler warned Jackie. "If you must fight I'll put you in a prize ring and you can earn some money doing it. The same goes for anybody else."

Several of the writers at Vero Beach sharply criticized Chandler for singling out Robinson. They claimed that Jackie was displaying an aggressive temperament that characterized many of the great players in baseball history, such as Ty Cobb, Frankie Frisch, Pepper Martin, Enos Slaughter, Phil Cavaretta and dozens of others.

To warn Robinson against aggressive behavior, they argued, was to leave him open to attack, while figuratively tying his hands for defense.

However, this was a new Robinson, needing no support from the sports writers. Jackie was like a gamecock that had been tied to a stake and taunted and tortured to a bristling edge. He was not only ready to fight his own battles, he was ready to start them.

The writers traveling with the Dodgers sensed the change in Jackie. In 1947 he had been forced by expediency to adopt a humble, apologetic, submissive attitude. For survival, he was required to submerge completely his naturally contentious nature. He had to face himself daily in the mirror and see a flesh-and-blood caricature of the type of Negro that was anathema to him.

Some hint of his true personality came through in 1948, particularly during the spring training squabble with Durocher and the sports writers, and the baiting later in the season of umpire Henline which caused his first expulsion from a game.

But in 1949 this was Jackie Robinson unfettered and unafraid. This was Jackie Robinson who had proved his ability to play major league baseball as a Negro, and who now demanded the right to play it as a man. He had reclaimed his very soul and his emotions from their two years in limbo. Now he was more than Jackie Robinson, the wizard with a glove, the electrifying runner of bases, the man with the big hit in his bat. He was Jackie Robinson, the hotheaded pop off, the poor loser, the acid-tongued agitator, the quick-tempered, blazing-eyed man with the big No. 42 on his back.

Take it or leave it. Like it or lump it.

The sports writers could not know all of this. But they could perceive a portion of it, enough to sharpen their pencils and wet their lips in anticipation as the Dodgers headed north for opening day at Ebbets Field.

A tumultuous, record-setting opening day crowd of 34,530 fans bulged into Ebbets Field to see the Dodgers and the Giants start the 1949 campaign rolling. The Dodgers were a vastly improved ball club over the 1948 aggregation, if for no other reason than that the confusion of multiple-position playing was largely avoided.

In 1948, with Robinson out of condition, there had been considerable shifting in and out of the line-up of the Dodgers' younger players. Gil Hodges defended part time at first and part time behind the plate, sharing the latter job with Roy Campanella. Duke Snider got into only fifty-three games. Robinson himself filled in occasionally at first base and third.

This time Shotton, at the helm from the beginning, settled his key players into position and gave them the benefit of daily competition. Hodges became the first baseman and Roy Campanella the regular catcher. Snider was given permanent possession of center field. Robinson and Reese were the flashiest double-play combination in baseball, and the Dodgers had a Negro rookie hurler named Don Newcombe added to the staff.

The results of opening day augured well for Brooklyn. Batting in the cleanup spot for the first time, Robinson started a four-run rally in the fourth inning with a home run. He added two singles to the homer later as the Dodgers went on to rout the Giants, 10–3.

Brooklyn was off and running, with Robinson leading the way. By the last week in May Jackie was banging the ball at a .331 clip. He had already slammed six home runs, half his total production of the year before. He was leading the league with thirty-four runs batted in.

Up to that point, all had been serene on the rhubarb front. The sports writers were patient. A Memorial Day double-header with the Giants was coming up. How long could Robinson and Durocher glare at each other without something popping?

True enough, the tightly fought first game of the double-header had Robinson and Durocher sniping at each other before it was half over. But Jackie won this round—in a typical Robinson fashion.

In the thirteenth inning of a 1–1 tie, Jackie cracked a home run off Dave Koslo to wrap up the game for Brooklyn.

The bench jockeying was resumed as the second game got under way. In the ninth inning, with the Giants leading, 7–4, Snider walked and Robinson forced him at second base. Durocher came up out of the dugout and called for a meeting on the mound. Catcher Mickey Livingston joined him, Buddy Kerr came over from shortstop and Bill Rigney from second.

Robinson hadn't noticed whether or not the umpires had officially called time. In case they hadn't and the ball was still in play, he wasn't going to let a vacant second base stare him in the face. He lit out for the bag, but time had, indeed, been called and the umpires waved him back to first.

As he trotted back, the Giant bench hooted at him, "Nifty steal, there, Jackie." "Why didn't you slide, Robbie?"

Catcher Livingston, standing with the group at the mound, stepped aside, gestured with his mask at Jackie and let loose a few choice digs of his own.

Jackie yelled back at Livingston. Then, when Durocher left the mound and started for the Giant dugout, Robinson switched his attack to Leo. Durocher replied in kind, and while the next two Dodgers were making out to end the ball game, the two men continued their abuse of each other.

With the game over, Jackie walked off first base and headed for the clubhouse in center field. As he walked, he kept his head turned in Durocher's direction, still hurling insults. The Giant manager headed in Jackie's direction, but the chance of anything further developing vanished in a sudden uproar as a youngster leaped out of the stands, grabbed Frankie Frisch's cap and sped away, with Frisch and several park police in pursuit.

In the Giant clubhouse moments later, an indignant Leo Durocher threw down the gauntlet. "I didn't even say a word to Robinson," Leo protested his innocence. "Livingston was on him, not me. Then all of a sudden I hear him giving me the business. All I did then was motion to the dugout that Robinson had a big head these days.

"But as long as that's the way he wants it, I'll give it to him—but good, from now on."

From now on, as it turned out, was to run a long time, until Durocher retired from baseball in 1955. Each year the feud was renewed, often reaching bitter heights. Yet, strangely enough, each man had tremendous respect for the other's abilities.

Robinson, in the meantime, seemed to be feuding with half the pitchers in the National League. Or at least the pitchers, for their part, were in a belligerent frame of mind. Jackie was being "brushed back" with discouraging regularity by hurlers from every team in the league.

There was a kind of vicious cycle to it. The more Jackie was thrown at and knocked down by pitches whistling past his ear, the quicker he was to bounce up, spit a string of invectives at the hurler and rap the next pitch for a base hit. And the more he hit, the more they threw at him.

In June Jackie took over the league batting leadership with a .348 average. In July he moved it up to .350, to .360. Early that month, his old enemies the Philadelphia Phillies lit into him again. It was at a night game in Ebbets Field. The Phillies, though coasting all the way through the game with a substantial lead, had been riding the Dodgers—and Jackie in particular—all night.

In the sixth inning, with the Phillies ahead 7–2, Robinson stepped to the plate. From the Philadelphia dugout came the raucous shouting of relief pitcher Schoolboy Rowe, calling to the Phillies' hurler at the moment, Ken Heintzelman.

"Throw at him, Kenny. Knock him down!"

Robinson stepped out of the batter's box momentarily and turned to catcher Stan Lopata. "Listen to that washed-up bum. That's all he's good for now, collecting splinters on the bench and hollering at what the other guy should do. If he was out there now he wouldn't even have the guts to throw at me."

Apparently Lopata related to Rowe between innings what Robinson had said. The next time Jackie came to bat, the catcher said to him, "Rowe said why don't you say that to his face?"

Robinson stepped out of the box, cupped his hands around his mouth and called out to Rowe on the bench, "Rowe, I meant every word I said!"

Rowe leaped out of the dugout, but immediately plate umpire Artie Gore rushed in front of him.

"Back into the dugout, Rowe," the umpire barked.

The pitcher made a move to get around Gore. The umpire stuck out his hand. "You don't hop right back down there and I'll throw you out of the game and report you to the commissioner."

By the end of July, Robinson was leading the

163

league in almost every important offensive department—average, total hits, runs scored, runs batted in, stolen bases, sacrifices and two-base hits.

Moving into the month of August, it was apparent that the pennant race was a Dodgers-Cardinals duel. At the moment the Red Birds were holding a slight lead, but they were running with the hot breath of the Dodgers continually on their necks. And every time they looked back, they could see the challenging grin of Jackie Robinson.

In Philadelphia one day in August, Jackie won a game with a two-out, three-run home run in the ninth inning.

The Cardinal players, reading the story in the St. Louis papers the next day, shook their heads ruefully. "That Robinson," one of them said. "If it wasn't for him the Dodgers would be in the second division."

The others murmured agreement. "The thing about Robbie," shortstop Marty Marion said admiringly, "is that he can find more ways to beat you. He'll hit the home run one time, then bunt and run you crazy the next. He keeps you on edge, especially the pitchers. He's always up to something."

That same month Robinson strained a ligament in his right foot. The injury required rest, but this was no time to rest. He knew he couldn't be spared. Playing became a daily ordeal of agony for Jackie, and the injury was being aggravated by the extra strain put upon it.

His play fell off sharply in September. He admitted to a sports writer that he could use a few days rest, but he wouldn't ask to be taken out. At the same time, Manager Shotton had no intentions of doing the asking himself. The way Shotton felt about it, a one-legged Robinson was better than no Robinson at all.

Not a few of the Dodger players felt the same way about Jackie. "We'll never win it without Robbie in there every day," one of them declared. "Just his being out at second, in the line-up, gives you the feeling that you can pull any game out of the fire."

"How many times this season," another agreed, "has Robbie started a winning rally with a hit, or a stolen base, or a walk? You have the feeling that as long as Jackie has another lick coming, anything can happen."

Then the Dodgers moved into St. Louis for a three-game series that could decide the pennant. The Cardinals were still in front by a game and a half. On the twenty-first, there was a day-night double-header scheduled.

Don Newcombe opposed Max Lanier in the afternoon game. To add tension to the already electric atmosphere in Sportsman's Park, both pitchers were at their superb best that day. The game went into the bottom of the ninth inning a scoreless tie.

Newcombe threw two quick strikes past St. Louis lead-off man Enos Slaughter. The next pitch plate umpire Bill Stewart called a ball. Newcombe howled at the call. So did Campanella. So did Robinson. On the next pitch Slaughter doubled to left field.

Ron Northey was purposely walked, and Bill Howerton bunted safely to load the bases with nobody out.

Robinson began walking toward the mound, ostensibly to calm Newcombe. Campanella also began walking toward the Dodger pitcher. Suddenly Robinson looked significantly at umpire Stewart, put his fingers to his throat in the recognized baseball gesture for "choking up"—losing nerve in a tense situation—and began talking to Newcombe and Campanella.

"Boy, did Stewart blow that third strike call on Slaughter," Jackie growled.

At first Stewart didn't notice Jackie's gestures. But when Robinson continued to make the "choke up" signs after he'd gone back to his second base position, he caught the umpire's attention.

Stewart tore off his mask and stepped out in front of the plate. His right arm jerked right up in the air. "You're out of the game, Robinson!" he called.

At once Robinson, Reese, Newcombe, Campanella and coaches Milt Stock, Jake Pitler and Clyde Sukeforth surrounded the umpire, protesting the ejection of the Dodgers' key player in such a tight spot of a crucial game. Stewart was adamant, however.

"He's out of the game—and that's all."

Robinson pushed forward belligerently. "That proves it, Stewart!" he yelled at the umpire. "That proves you choked up! You know you blew that third strike on Slaughter! If you didn't know it you wouldn't be throwing me out of here!"

The Dodger coaches dragged Jackie away from Stewart before he could say or do something that would warrant a suspension. It was tough enough losing him now with the bases loaded against them and nobody out.

When play was resumed, Joe Garagiola hit Newcombe's first pitch for a single to win the game, 1–0.

Fortunately for Brooklyn, Preacher Roe shut out the Cardinals in the night game, 5–0. The Dodgers were still one and a half games out of first place.

With little more than a week remaining to the season, the Cardinals began printing their World Series tickets. But as happens so often in sports, while the overconfident team is dreaming of spending the winner's spoils, its rival is running off with the loot.

The Cardinals dropped four straight games to

the sixth-place Pirates and the last-place Cubs. On the final day of the season, the Dodgers led by one game. The Cardinals won their last game quickly, and the result was posted on the scoreboard during the Dodgers-Phillies battle.

If the Dodgers lost this game, there would be a play-off for the pennant. In 1946 the Dodgers and Cardinals had been forced into a play-off, the Cardinals winning in two straight games. Brooklyn wanted no opportunity for a repeat performance by the Red Birds.

The Dodgers had to go to the tenth inning to nail it down. They scored twice in that frame to beat the Phillies, 9–7, and capture the National League flag.

The 1949 World Series had few moments of cheer either for the Dodgers or for Jackie Robinson. Their by now traditional Fall Classic rivals, the New York Yankees, took the World's Championship in five games. The Dodgers got pretty fair pitching, but inadequate hitting.

Jackie himself hit safely only three times in sixteen trips; in addition, he immersed himself in hot water again for criticizing an umpire.

In the Dodger dressing room after the first game of the series, won by the Yankees 1–0, Jackie complained about the calls of plate umpire Cal Hubbard.

"I've never seen such bad strikes called," he fumed. "He actually called one pitchout a strike."

Later, when he had cooled off, Robinson told reporters he wanted to make a public apology. "I lost my head," he said. "We were beaten legitimately, and I thought, all in all, Hubbard called a good game."

But Commissioner Happy Chandler was not quite satisfied with Jackie's apology. He sent word to Manager Shotton that he expected better behavior from Robinson. He said he wanted Robinson to stop "popping off" at the umpires.

Jackie accepted the rebuke calmly. But he wasn't making any promises.

A month later, the first Negro to play major league baseball, the first Negro to play in a World Series, became the first Negro to win the Most Valuable Player award, voted for and presented by the Baseball Writers Association.

In earning the award, Jackie had won the league batting title with a .342 average. He led in stolen bases with 37, hit 16 home runs, batted in 124 runs, scored 122. He tied a National League record by playing in 156 games at second base in one season, and led the league's second basemen in double plays. In the annual All-Star game in July, he had been selected to play second base for the National League.

Two more prized awards came Jackie's way before the year was out. Both were for his contributions to human relations, rather than the Dodgers' pennant chase. On December 13th the United States Maccabi Association and the Manischewitz Foundation presented Jackie with the Benny Leonard good sportsmanship trophy, "for courage, for fair play, and for interest in humanity."

The next day Robinson received the 1949 George Washington Carver Memorial Institute gold medal for his "contribution to the betterment of race relations."

And still the honors came. In January, *Sport Magazine* named Jackie baseball's "Top Performer of the Year," and New York's Uptown Chamber of Commerce awarded him a bronze plaque for "outstanding work in the field of race relations." Then the alumni of UCLA, Jackie's alma mater, voted him one of the school's all-time great halfbacks.

Finally, on January 24th, Branch Rickey awarded Jackie a 1950 contract calling for upward of thirty-five thousand dollars, making Robinson, at the time, one of the highest paid Dodgers in Brooklyn history.

CHAPTER SEVENTEEN

INJURIES and umpires plagued Jackie Robinson in 1950. Although he sat out only ten games during the season, from opening day on, Jackie was playing below his physical par. It began in spring training with a badly twisted ankle.

"I can't take time out to rest it," Jackie told trainer Doc Wendler. "I'll never get into shape in time for opening day, so I'll just have to try to play on it. Tape it tight for me, will you?"

Favoring the right foot cut down on Jackie's base-running antics, but it seemed to have no effect on his batting. Then, sliding home against the Giants one day in July, he slammed into catcher Wes Westrum, who was blocking the plate. Jackie was safe, but he rose to his feet painfully and limped back into the Dodger dugout.

Three days later he had to keep himself out of the game for the first time. The left knee, which he had injured sliding into Westrum, had stiffened to the point where he couldn't bend the joint. The combination of injured right ankle and left knee made fielding next to impossible. Jackie had no choice but to sit out until the knee, at least, loosened enough for him to bend it.

Several weeks later Robinson pulled a muscle in his left thigh. Since it didn't slow him down enough to warrant his being benched, he played out the injury. Shortly afterward he was hit in the left elbow with a pitch thrown by Bob Rush of the Cubs.

The elbow swelled and stiffened. After a week he could barely bend the arm, and then only with severe pain. Jackie's concession to the injury was the suggestion to Manager Shotton that he hit seventh in the batting order for a while, instead of cleanup.

During the stretch drive in early September, in the midst of battling the Phillies for the pennant, Jackie made a diving stop of a ground ball with his gloved hand. He made the out, but jammed his left thumb into the ground and was forced out of the game an inning later when the thumb suddenly swelled like a fiery balloon.

There was no fracture, but X rays revealed badly torn tendons. His left hand was placed in a splint, and the doctors estimated that he'd be out of action for three weeks.

"Impossible," Jackie protested. "That would mean the rest of the season." A week later he had the splint removed, a special rubberized protector put on the thumb, and he trotted out to second base.

But this was Philadelphia's year. The "Whiz Kids," as the young Phillies team was termed that season, slugged it out with the Dodgers down the home stretch, and beat them on the last day to win the pennant.

For most of the season, Jackie had been sparring with the umpires. From his second base position, he had fallen into the habit of calling the pitches along with the umpire. He frequently disagreed with the official's call. Then, on July 2nd, batting against Curt Simmons of the Phillies, Robinson took a called third strike.

As he started to walk away, plate umpire Jocko Conlan said to him, "That strike was right down the middle. Right down the middle."

Jackie turned angrily and said something to Conlan, and the umpire jerked off his mask and gestured with his right thumb. "Get out of the game," he snarled.

"Get out?" protested Jackie. "Listen, Conlan—" he began, but coach Clyde Sukeforth was already there to pull him away.

In the clubhouse later, Robinson complained bitterly about his ejection. "Sure, I said something

Conlan didn't like, but it wasn't anything a hundred other guys don't say to umpires when they get sore. And I had a right to be sore. Where does an umpire come off riding a player? Wasn't it bad enough I took a third strike without Conlan reminding me of it?"

"The umpires have gotten too powerful," Jackie added. "Something's going to have to be done about it."

Six days later, while Robinson was sitting out a game at Ebbets Field with his knee injury, the Dodger bench began riding plate umpire Lou Jorda. In the sixth inning, Jorda wheeled suddenly and pointed to the Dodger dugout.

"Robinson! Out! Off the bench!" he called.

Jackie was stunned for a moment. "Me? What for?"

"You know what for! Let's go! Off the bench!"

In the clubhouse after the game, it was coach Clyde Sukeforth, rather than Robinson, who was storming. "They're ganging up on Jackie. Jorda had the wrong guy this time—and he knows it. Everybody else on the bench was yelling but not Jackie this time. It so happens that at exactly that moment Jackie wasn't saying anything because Shotton was telling him he would be up next to pinch-hit.

"There's no doubt the umpires are ganging up on him. It's an unhealthy situation," the coach continued his protest. "They have no boss. They're riding over everybody. Everybody is disciplined but the umpires."

Sukeforth's charges were strong enough to arouse Ford Frick, the National League president. He told newsmen that he would confer personally with Robinson and Sukeforth about the situation. Frick admitted, much to Robinson's surprise, that umpire Jocko Conlan had been "guilty of hasty action" in ejecting Robinson the week before, after riding him about striking out.

Frick's intervention stopped the summary ejections by quick-triggered umpires. At the same time, however, he advised Robinson to quit badgering the umpires on ball and strike calls.

One of the amazing accomplishments of Jackie that otherwise undistinguished season was that despite his constant run of injuries, he led the league's second basemen in fielding, with a .986 average, and established a new National League record for double plays by a second baseman with one hundred and thirty-three. For the second straight year he was selected to play second base on the National League All-Star team.

At the plate, Jackie hit .328, with fourteen home runs and eighty-one runs batted in. The most noticeable effect of his injuries appeared in the base-stealing department. Jackie stole only twelve bases.

As sorry as Jackie was to lose the pennant that

year, he was even sorrier to lose Branch Rickey. After the World Series, the Dodger president announced that he had sold his interest in the Dodgers and was moving to Pittsburgh.

"I owe too much to Rickey," said Robinson, "to even try to explain how I feel about his leaving Brooklyn. It's sure going to feel funny playing my head off trying to beat him, but that's baseball," Jackie sighed.

Rickey had no illusions about Pittsburgh. There was a monumental rebuilding job to be done on the Pirates. There was no conflict of interest, therefore, when, in his departing speech to the press, he predicted that the Dodgers would win the pennant in 1951, and that Robinson would have one of his most spectacular years.

Spectacular was the word for it. When Jackie signed his 1951 contract with Walter O'Malley, the new Dodger president, he said he intended to get off to a fast start that year. And he kept his word.

He was thrown out of a game by an umpire before the regular season even opened.

It was only an exhibition game at Asheville, North Carolina, but that didn't make Jackie want to win it any the less. In the fifth inning he hit a ground ball to third, and thought he had beaten the throw to first base. But umpire Frank Dascoli called him out.

Jackie turned back toward the bench, muttering

about the decision. Then he turned and said something to Dascoli. The umpire, who later claimed Jackie had been profane, immediately waved his arms and threw Jackie out of the game.

Considering that it happened in an exhibition game, it may properly be considered a prelude to the fireworks that were to come during the regular season.

Before the start of the opening game, Charley Dressen, the new Dodger manager, took Jackie aside and made a deal with him.

"Listen, Robbie," the skipper said, "I know you got a right to beef against bad calls the same as anybody else. Only I got a tip that the umps are going to be on your tail this year even worse than they were last year. They're claiming you're trying to show them up."

Jackie started to protest, but Dressen cut him off.

"Okay, okay, I know it isn't so, but the thing is we can't have you getting kicked out of the game all the time. Now you try the hardest to keep your mouth shut, and I'll back you up when you got a beef. Soon as you start squawking out there I'm going to run out and take over. And when I do I want you to keep quiet. It's okay if I get the heave ho, but I want you playing, not sitting on the bench."

"I'll try," Jackie agreed. "I'll try to keep my mouth shut."

"Heck, Robbie," Dressen said, "you did the first year and a half you were up—and things were tougher for you then. Why can't you do it now?"

"That's just why I can't, Charley," Jackie said. "Or to be honest, maybe it's why I don't try. I keep remembering what I took with my mouth shut for a year and a half."

Jackie's first run-in with an umpire came during opening week of the 1951 season. Called out on strikes by umpire Dusty Boggess, Robinson tossed his bat away angrily and trotted out to second base, shouting an acrimonious remark at Boggess. The plate umpire coolly turned away and ignored the outburst.

But third base umpire Babe Pinelli chose not to ignore it. He stomped over to Jackie and berated him for his remarks.

Robinson blew up. "Who was talking to you, Pinelli? What are you butting in for if I got a beef with Boggess?"

Pinelli flew right back at him, and the two stood snarling belligerently at each other. In a flash Dressen was on the scene. He gently shoved Jackie out of the way and took over the argument, just in time to save Jackie from being ejected.

On April 30th the Dodgers took on the Giants in a night game at Ebbets Field. The rivalry between these two clubs had been a bitter one for years. And now the Giants were in a quarrelsome

178

mood. They had lost eleven straight games and were in last place.

The Giants couldn't think of a team they would rather vent their anger upon than the Dodgers. And with that in mind they sent to the mound their ace Dodger killer Sal Maglie, "The Barber."

Young Chris Van Cuyk started for Brooklyn, but he didn't get past the first inning. The Giants shelled him out with a six-run outburst, then settled down to watch Maglie toy with the Dodgers.

It wasn't one of Sal's better nights. Gene Hermanski led off against him with a home run. Two outs later, Robinson hit another home run. By the third inning, the score was 8–3 in favor of the Giants. With two out, Robinson came to bat again.

Jackie walked to the plate slowly, with his pigeon-toed gait, and dug in at the batter's box. He wagged his bat back and forth several times, then nervously rubbed his right hand along his trouser leg.

Maglie scowled down at him behind his blue-black beard, then wound up and threw a fast ball inside. Robinson leaped back to avoid being hit. Jackie looked out at the mound, then stepped back in. Maglie spun and threw, and again Robinson was forced to jump back out of the way.

On the next pitch, Jackie swiveled around and dropped a bunt down the first base line. Maglie broke for the ball, then eased up near the base line as he saw the ball twisting away foul.

But Jackie never stopped running. He came barreling down the line and rammed Maglie as he would have blocked out a man in his football days at UCLA. Maglie staggered back, then charged at Robinson. Eddie Stanky, who had gone over to cover first on the bunt play, ran in and grabbed Maglie and Durocher rushed off the bench to help.

Jackie calmly turned and walked slowly back to the batter's box. As he settled into position once more, catcher Wes Westrum spoke to him. "Sal wasn't throwing at you, Jack. But you've been wearing us out. He was just trying to brush you back."

Robinson glared at him. "That's too fine a difference for me," he growled. Then he rapped Maglie's next pitch for a single to center.

The Giants won the ball game without further incident, but the Robinson-Maglie affair kicked up a king-size storm in the National League president's office. President Ford Frick called Buzzy Bavasi, the Dodger vice-president, and told him flatly to curb Robinson's aggressiveness.

"I'm tired of him popping off and second guessing the umpires and all the rest of the stuff that went on last night. If the Brooklyn club can't handle him, I will."

The Dodger front office publicly defended Jackie. President Walter O'Malley told the New York sports writers, "I have no reason to be dissatisfied with Jackie Robinson, his conduct on the field or his spirit—and I have seen all the games at Ebbets Field and at the Polo Grounds. Jackie has the full support of this organization."

Vice-president Bavasi charged that Frick was warning the wrong team and the wrong man. "If he wants to bring Jackie on the carpet, he should also bring in Larry Jansen and Leo Durocher. After all, it was Jansen who started the fuss by hitting Jackie with a pitched ball the day before."

Jackie didn't let the uproar affect his play, however. The next day against the Pirates he hit a single and a triple to boost his average to .389.

For the first time since the year he broke into major league baseball, Robinson received a death threat. While the Dodgers were in Cincinnati, the police and the Cincinnati *Enquirer* got identical letters in the mail warning that Robinson would be shot if he played at Crosley Field.

While the notes were believed to be the work of a crank, the FBI and local police took no chances. They spread out through the stands during the day's game and stationed men on rooftops surrounding the ball park.

Jackie, as a matter of fact, regarded the threat more lightly than he did an affront to his hitting ability during the game. In the seventh inning, with the Dodgers holding a slim 4–3 lead, Cal Abrams singled and Reese sacrificed. Cincinnati manager Luke Sewell ordered Duke Snider intentionally walked to get to Robinson.

Robinson was really burned. There were thousands of Negro fans, he knew, who traveled regularly to Cincinnati from as far away as Alabama and Tennessee, when the Dodgers came to town. He knew this had nothing to do with Sewell's decision to walk Snider and pitch to him, but just the same he felt it was a direct challenge.

It was poor strategy on Sewell's part. A member of the New York Giants had remarked earlier that year, "Durocher's a terrific manager, but he always makes the same mistake. He gets Robinson sore at us. That's the wrong thing to do with Robinson."

Jackie never proved the truth of the statement better than he did that moment at Crosley Field. He whacked pitcher Ewell Blackwell's second serve over the left field fence for a home run.

It was in that fantastic year of 1951, too, that Jackie came his closest to an actual fist fight with another player. The man was Philadelphia pitcher Russ Meyer, one of the few men then in baseball possessed of a quicker temper than Jackie Robinson's.

By the eighth inning of the Dodgers-Phillies night game at Ebbets Field on May 31st, Meyer was tired and crotchety. The Dodgers were leading, 3–2. Meyer's control had been off all night. He was sweaty and angry at himself and irritated at the umpires' calls. Eight Dodgers had walked thus far.

Robinson led off the Dodger eighth with a single. Then he stole second, which pushed Meyer a little farther toward the edge. Russ hit Hodges with a pitch, then with Furillo at bat he delivered a wild pitch and Robinson sped to third.

On the next serve Manager Dressen signaled for a squeeze play. Robinson charged down off third, but Furillo missed the pitch. Jackie put on the brakes halfway between third and home, and the Phillies started a rundown on Robinson. Jackie jockeyed back and forth along the line, but they couldn't get the tag on him. The crowd was bellowing its enjoyment of Jackie's skill as the Phillies chased him fruitlessly.

Finally, Jackie broke past catcher Andy Seminick and streaked for the plate. Meyer, backing up the play, took the throw from the third baseman, but dropped it as Jackie ran into him in front of home plate. Robinson was safe!

Instantly Meyer charged at Jackie, his fists cocked. He thrust his head forward and screamed that Jackie had pushed him and knocked the ball out of his hand. Robinson yelled right back at him.

Players poured from both dugouts. The Phillies' Jimmy Bloodworth grabbed Meyer bodily and pulled him away. Manager Eddie Sawyer wisely told Meyer to cool off, then replaced him with Jim Konstanty.

But it wasn't over yet. Meyer stalked into the Philadelphia dugout, his face flaming. Slamming his glove on the bench, he turned and yelled across at Robinson, sitting in the Dodger dugout. Then he motioned to Jackie and headed for the runway under the stands.

Jackie jumped off the bench and ducked down the steps to meet the pitcher's challenge. But players streamed down the steps after them and broke it up before the two men could meet.

After the game, which the Dodgers won, Meyer and Robinson got together and shook hands. Russ apologized for losing his temper, and Jackie said he'd made a mistake by accepting Meyer's challenge for a meeting under the stands.

By midsummer, it appeared that the pennant race was all over. On August 11th, the Dodgers were leading the second-place Giants by thirteen and a half games.

But the already turbulent season was due for an absolutely hysterical finish.

CHAPTER EIGHTEEN

On August 12th Al Corwin and Larry Jansen of the Giants beat the Philadelphia Phillies in a double-header. That started it. The Giants went on a sixteen-game winning streak that didn't end until the Giants had drawn to within six games of the league-leading Brooklyn Dodgers. It was an impressive string of victories, but with only four weeks of the season remaining, nobody attached much significance to it.

Little by little, day by day, the Giants inched closer to Brooklyn. Five games behind, four games, three. The pressure was on the Dodgers now. To lose the pennant after holding a seemingly insurmountable lead would be a calamity. Now Brooklyn's lead was cut to two games. One and a half. Back to two. Then one. Then came the celebrated rhubarb at Boston on September 27th.

The score was tied 3–3 in the eighth inning. With

Bob Addis on third for Boston, a slow ground ball was hit at Robinson. Addis headed for the plate. Jackie charged the ball and threw to Campanella. Addis slid into the Dodger catcher in a cloud of dust. Umpire Frank Dascoli, hovering over the play, called Addis safe.

The Dodgers roared in outrage. Campanella leaped into the air in disgust, then slammed his mitt to the ground right in front of Dascoli. Coach Cookie Lavagetto and pitcher Preacher Roe stormed to the plate, both shouting their protest at the call.

As the argument flared, Dascoli threw Campanella out of the game. Then he ordered Lavagetto out. The Dodger players on the bench started yelling at Dascoli and he ordered the entire bench cleared of Dodgers except for Manager Dressen.

That was the way the game ended, 4–3 Boston, and the Dodger lead over the Giants was now a bare half game.

When the four umpires ducked under the stands after the game, heading for their dressing room, they were met by Campanella, in his street clothes, and a group of angry Brooklyn players. The Dodgers cut loose at Dascoli with a barrage of vitriol, and they didn't spare the language.

What they were protesting, more than the decision at the plate, was the ejection of Campanella from such an important and closely contested ball game. Most sports wirters, the next day, sided with

186

the Dodgers on this issue, claiming, as the Dodgers did, that Dascoli should have made allowances for Campanella's outburst under the strained circumstances of the moment.

For as it turned out, when the Dodgers batted in the ninth inning, they got a man to third base with Campanella's place in the batting order up next. So instead of a man batting .327 hitting in that clutch spot, there was Wayne Terwilliger, pinch-hitting—with a .227 average. The run never scored.

The four umpires managed to push their way through the angry group of Dodgers and locked themselves in their dressing room. The Brooklyn players remained in the runway, continuing their attack on Dascoli.

While his teammates shrieked insults at the umpires, one of the Dodgers began pounding on the dressing room door with his fists. Then, as the Dodgers turned toward their own locker room, the player kicked the door viciously, splintering one of the panels.

The Dodger player accused of kicking the door was Jackie Robinson. He was summarily fined one hundred dollars by Ford Frick, who also fined Campanella one hundred dollars and Preacher Roe fifty dollars. Jackie declared his innocence. "Whenever I'm in a crowd and something happens," he complained, "right away they blame me." He knew who had actually splintered the umpires' door, but turning the player in was unthinkable.

Jackie's story was backed up by Preacher Roe. "I was there and I saw who did it," the Dodger hurler said. "It wasn't Jackie. I'll take an oath on that."

Roe was on perfectly safe ground. It was Preacher himself who had done the kicking. He revealed this himself, many years later, telling how much he admired Robinson for taking the fine without a squawk, when he knew all the time who the culprit was.

Incredibly, on the final day of the season, the Dodgers and the Giants were tied for first place. The Dodgers' lead of thirteen and a half games had vanished completely. They were in Philadelphia now for their last game, while the Giants were to play Boston.

The Polo Grounders, continuing their fantastic pace, beat the Braves, 3–2, while the Dodgers were still in the throes of a desperate struggle in Philadelphia. In the Giant clubhouse after their game, the players sat around in their uniforms and listened to a special radio broadcast of the contest from Philadelphia.

The Dodgers were losing, 6–2. There was a runner on base and Jackie Robinson stepped up to hit. "Don't let this guy get a good one," one of the Giant players muttered. But Jackie ripped a tremendous triple to left center field and the score was 6–3.

A Giant player shouted in admiration. "That Robinson!"

Two more runs crossed for the Dodgers, and it was a 6–5 ball game. Then the Phillies scored twice in their half of the inning to make it 8–5. The Giant players were jubilant. The pennant was minutes away now.

At that moment in Philadelphia, the scoreboard posted the Giant victory over the Braves. The Dodgers, with that specter on the scoreboard reminding them that there were no more tomorrows, came to bat in the eighth inning and grimly battered three runs over the plate to tie the score.

It was unbelievable. The excitement, the tension, the high stakes, the drama of the entire baseball season concentrated into these few moments comprised a plot a fiction writer wouldn't dare develop.

Now, in the ninth inning, with the score tied, the rival managers brought their ace pitchers in from the bull pen. Robin Roberts took the mound for the Phillies, Don Newcombe would pitch the bottom of the ninth for Brooklyn. Both men had toiled the night before, Newcombe winning, 5–0. But this was the time for the best pitching available, inning by inning. The men would have all winter to rest their weary arms.

The game went into extra innings. The two great moundsmen reached into the depths of their reserve strength as they toiled through the tenth, the eleventh. Suddenly in the twelfth Newcombe weakened. The Phillies loaded the bases with two out. To the plate strode Eddie Waitkus.

In the locker room of the New York Giants the players sat limply. Silently they urged Waitkus to break up the game.

Don Newcombe shook off the weariness that sagged his shoulders and pitched to the Phillies' first baseman. Waitkus swung—and cracked a low line drive past Newcombe headed for right center field. It was a certain hit.

Robinson streaked toward second at the crack of the bat. Desperation churned his legs like pistons. At the last split second he hurled his body through the air at the speeding white pellet, both arms straining from their sockets.

The ball plunked into the pocket of Jackie's glove for one of the most incredibly sensational catches in the history of baseball.

But as Robinson's body hit the ground full force, his elbow jammed into the pit of his stomach. It was like being hit with a sledge hammer. For the moment Jackie blacked out, but he held onto the ball. Then a searing pain spread through his chest. He couldn't breathe. He lay there on the ground back of second, gasping for air like a fish out of water. And he tried not to cry.

The tears came to his eyes from the pain, and he

hadn't the strength to hold them back. Pee Wee Reese came over from shortstop and quietly took the ball from Robinson's glove. Then he signaled for the Dodger trainer.

Jackie couldn't even talk. He pointed silently to his stomach. The Dodger trainer loosened Jackie's clothing and gently massaged the muscles. Robinson took a long swallow of water, and after a few moments he was able to stand up. The cheers and the applause for a great competitor filled Shibe Park—Shibe Park, where only four years earlier Jackie Robinson had been subjected to the most humiliating racial abuse.

Jackie continued in the game. The pain in his stomach and chest persisted and his knees were wobbly, but he played on. As the Dodgers came to bat in the fourteenth inning Jackie felt he couldn't go on. Nausea was beginning to tear at him. He felt washed out. Due to bat third in the inning, he felt it would be better to have a man pinch-hit for him.

But by the time he made up his mind to tell Dressen, Reese and Snider were retired and it was his turn to bat. Somehow he found himself at home plate with a bat in his hand. Roberts cranked up and threw, and Jackie swung at the first pitch.

Every person in the ball park knew it from the crack of the bat. A deafening roar filled the stadium. The Dodger players leaped off the bench and swung each other in the air. Jackie ran easily around the bases with the home run that won the game—that sent the Dodgers into a pennant play-off with the Giants.

And the Giants, sitting in the locker room, still in their grimy uniforms, shook their heads in disbelief and stared at the radio. Then one of them strode over and twisted the knob savagely. "What are you gonna do with that Robinson!" he said wonderingly.

After one of the most thrilling finishes in the annals of baseball, it hardly seemed possible that the Dodgers and Giants could provide even greater excitement. The partisan followers of both teams were already weak from the heart-stopping finale in Philadelphia. But there was more to come.

The three-game pennant play-off opened in Brooklyn, with Jim Hearn winning for the Giants, 3–1. The scene switched to the Polo Grounds. In the first inning Reese singled and with two out, Jackie socked a home run over the left field wall for a 2–0 lead. In the fifth inning Snider doubled and Jackie singled him home to make the score 3–0. From there the Dodgers broke the game open, winning 10–0.

All the chips were on the table now. No more play-offs. No more tomorrows and no more yesterdays. In a couple of hours you'd be a hero or an also-ran. It was Newcombe versus Maglie and then wait till next year.

Sal, the Dodger killer, opened shakily. He got Furillo, then walked Reese and Snider. Robinson started for the batter's box. Catcher Westrum called time and walked out to talk to Maglie. Jackie stood off to the side and waited for Westrum to return behind the plate.

This was Jackie's only baseball habit bordering on superstition. Most players have some habit of dress or procedure they adhere to rigidly. Some always drop their glove on the field in the same place. Some make it a point to step on the foul line going to and returning from their position. With one player it's the same seat on the bench; another will touch first base on the way to the outfield.

This was Jackie's oddity. He always stepped into the batter's box by walking across the plate in front of the catcher. If the Dodger dugout was on the third base side in a particular ball park, he would circle around the catcher and cross back in front of him from the first base side.

So he waited now until Westrum came back to squat behind the plate, then he stepped in with Reese on second and Snider on first. Maglie went into his stretch, came down to Jackie with a curve over the outside corner for a strike. Robinson wiggled his bat and nervously ran his right hand along his trouser leg—another Robinson trademark.

The count went to two balls and one strike. Maglie stretched, threw, and Jackie cracked it on a line to left center for a single. Reese wheeled around third base and charged home for a 1–0 lead. Clutch hitting—one more Robinson habit.

The score remained 1–0 through six innings. Maglie settled down and Newcombe was superb. The Giants tied the score in the seventh, but Brooklyn rocked Maglie with three in the eighth. Thus it was 4–1 Brooklyn as the Giants came to bat in the bottom of the ninth.

Grinning Dodger fans hooted and hollered at dejected Giant partisans heading for the exits.

Al Dark led off the Giants' last stand. Big Newcombe, appearing stronger than ever, blazed two fast balls through for strikes. He wasted a curve, then came back with the fast ball. Dark jumped on it and banged it to right field for a single. Don Mueller followed with another hit to the same spot and Dark scooted to third.

Giant fans halted their "abandon ship" movement. Grins on Dodger fans turned to anxious smiles. It couldn't happen. After blowing a thirteen and one-half-game lead their Dodgers had been rescued from the brink of disaster by a miracle on the final day of the season. Now they were three outs away from victory and the abyss was yawning again. No! It couldn't happen!

But they saw it happen with their own eyes. And since it was a miracle that had saved the Dodgers, it was perhaps fitting that another miracle should push them over the edge.

Monte Irvin stepped up to the plate. Newcombe mopped his forehead with the sleeve of his sweat shirt. He stretched and looked back at the runners. He pitched—and Irvin hit a high, twisting foul near the first base boxes. Hodges got the angle on it, tracked it to the railing and grabbed it for the first out.

A great sigh swept through the stands. The next moment it turned into a roar as Whitey Lockman doubled to left field. Dark scored and Mueller raced to third. It was 4–2 now. The tying runs were on the bases. The winning run was represented by Bobby Thomson, now walking slowly to the plate.

Time seemed to come to a standstill in New York. On the streets, in the shops, in offices, and factories and homes millions—yes, millions of citizens stopped what they were doing to listen to the radio or watch television as Thomson came to bat.

Clint Hartung was sent in by Durocher to run for Mueller, who had twisted his ankle sliding into third. Then Dodger manager Charley Dressen made a decision that was to be argued in baseball circles for years to come. He removed Newcombe and flagged in Ralph Branca from the Dodger bull pen.

The handsome young right-hander took his final warm-up pitches from the mound, hitched at his belt and signaled that he was ready. Campanella squatted to flash the sign and Thomson dug in.

Branca picked up the signal and delivered to the plate. It was a fast ball down the middle for a strike. A hush settled over the Polo Grounds as Branca peered down again for the sign from Campanella. No one moved. The refreshment hawkers stood in the stands silent as statues. The sports writers in the press box who had afternoon deadlines prepared alternate stories to be fed to their telegraphers the second the game was over.

Hartung inched down off third, Lockman off second. Branca took a full windup and threw another fast ball. Thomson swung. There was a crack of the bat, a split second of frozen silence, then a roar of amazement swelled into a deafening crescendo of sound as the ball sailed into the left field stands for the game and pennant-winning home run!

New York hadn't seen anything like it since V-E Day. Horns blew and whistles shrilled. People leaned out of windows and shouted the news to the streets. The Giants' television announcer was incoherent. Over and over again he shrieked into the microphone, "I don't believe it! I don't believe it!"

The Polo Grounds was a madhouse. Durocher and Stanky wrestled and hugged each other along the third base line. Veteran baseball writers leaned out of the press box and cheered. The players pounded each other and pummeled Thomson's back till it was sore.

The Dodgers disappeared silently into the darkness of the clubhouse.

CHAPTER NINETEEN

THE night was dark and moonless, but the first real snow of winter lay freshly in glistening drifts on the open fields and on the rooftops of the houses. It makes everything look so clean, the snow, thought Jackie Robinson. He was sitting by the big living room window of the Robinsons' comfortable home in St. Albans, Queens, watching the last straggling flakes of white dance their way to the ground.

Less than two weeks to Christmas, he mused. Before you know it I'll be packing for Vero Beach again. Jackie sighed. It was getting tougher each year working into shape. I'll be what—thirty-five next month? The muscles and the joints don't respond the way they do when you're a college kid.

His mind flicked for a moment back to his days at UCLA. It seemed like only yesterday, and yet it seemed so long ago it must have been in another lifetime. He remembered Uncle Burton and the little apartment the Robinson family had on Pepper Street in Pasadena. And how he and Rae hoped to have a little apartment of their own someday and have some kids.

He looked across the room at his wife. Rae had been so good for him, from the very first. She had traveled the long, thorny road with him. In his first year with Brooklyn she had seen him consumed by silent rages, and she had begged him to let loose at her, to scream and rave at her in order to provide a release for his pent-up anger. Jackie smiled to himself. Later she tried just as hard to shut him up. How many times since he emerged from his shell of passiveness in 1949 had he promised her he'd try to control his temper on the ball field?

Lately, she'd been after him, quietly, to retire from baseball. While he could still get out with pride, she meant. Did he want to stick around till he was called the "aging veteran," filling in here and there, maybe being traded from club to club, a "throw-in" guy to complete a deal?

No, he didn't want that. And it would never happen. He'd quit the day he thought he was no longer an important part of a ball club. He hadn't come to that yet. Though the first signs had been there the past season. Anyway, he wasn't ready financially to leave baseball. He needed that big pay check. Only this morning he and Rae had given a binder on that new house in Stamford, Connecticut.

It was going to be a beauty when it was finished. Should be, Jackie thought. It would cost him about sixty-five thousand dollars before he was through. This house they had here in St. Albans was just too small for them now, with Jackie, Jr., Sharon and David not all having rooms of their own.

No, I'm not ready to leave baseball. Not before I have something else to substitute for it that will give my family security. Besides, I had a great year. My best World Series.

Jackie shook his head. We just can't beat those Yankees in a World Series. That's really eating me. Before I get out of baseball that's one thing I've got to see. The Dodgers beating the Yankees in the series. He thought back a moment. He'd been in how many?—four series, all against the Yankees, and all lost to them. His pride didn't take to that kind of record.

Well, at least they had carried the Yankees to seven games in the 1952 series. That was a close call. They had come uncomfortably near blowing the pennant again to the Giants. He had hit only .308 that year, his lowest average since 1948, but it was still tops on the club.

Then this past season . . . well, in spring training he wouldn't have given a nickel for the Dodgers' pennant chance at first. The memory of what happened at Vero Beach in the spring of 1953 pained him as it came back to him now. He stared out at the snow, so clean and white, and after a while, in his mind's eye, he could see the graceful sway of the Florida palms . . .

The Dodgers' Vero Beach clubhouse was empty except for Jackie Robinson. He was sitting on a stool in front of his locker, absently working a fist into the pocket of his glove. Jackie was waiting for Pee Wee Reese, the Dodger captain. Reese, Jackie knew, must be aware of what was going on. He could help. There wasn't a man on the Dodgers who didn't respect Reese, who wouldn't listen to his advice. And Jackie was positive, too, exactly where Pee Wee stood in this business.

Robinson shook his head sadly. It was hard to believe, after all these years, that a thing like this could happen on the Dodgers. And innocently, he himself was partially the cause of it. He sighed heavily. Well—

He heard the door to the locker room open and turned around to greet Reese. The Dodger captain was in his street clothes. The Dodger players had long since dressed and gone back to the hotel. Jackie had asked Reese to meet him in the clubhouse after they'd all gone.

Reese was smiling faintly. "What's all the mystery, Robbie? Why'd you want me to meet you in here?"

"Because if any of the guys would see us talking together for any length of time, it would be worse than my not talking to you at all," Jackie said.

"You're talking in riddles, Robbie. But go ahead, what's up?"

Robinson drew a deep breath. "There's something going on around here I think you should know about—or maybe you already know about it?"

Reese made no reply.

Jackie smiled. "Okay. You want to hear it from me. Well, Pee Wee, it really gets me. I thought this kind of thing was all over years ago, especially on the Dodgers. But I guess it'll never stop completely. Not in our lifetime, at least.

"Crank letters, threatening letters, dirt from the bench jockeys, that stuff hardly bothers me any more. But when I hear and feel race prejudice from my own teammates again, well, frankly, I don't know what to do about it. It can't be ignored, the way I did when I broke in. There are too many Negroes on this club, all over baseball now."

Pee Wee nodded. "I've heard the remarks."

"Then you know who started them and why. And I thought that guy was on my side. Heck, he's been with the club since 1948."

202

Reese shrugged. "Cox is his friend. They're pretty close buddies."

"Nobody's trying to steal anything from Cox," Jackie flared. "I've said a hundred times in public I think Billy's the best third baseman in the business. If Dressen thinks Gilliam should play second and me third, is that our fault?"

"Of course not," Reese said. "This guy's sore because he figured Cox had the job nailed down this year—until they brought Gilliam up. Then that game the other day, there was Black in there pitching—and Campy and you and Gilliam, and this guy started muttering about 'them taking over.'"

Jackie nodded. "That's all some of the lunkheads around here need to get them started. One guy with a big mouth to lead them. Look, Pee Wee. It's not a personal question with me so much. I've handled and taken lots worse abuse than this. But if it continues it's going to split this team wide open. We won't be worth two cents out on the field."

"That's a fact," Reese agreed. "What do you think I can do about it?"

"All the guys think you're okay. I mean they know you're fair and they respect you. None of them would dare say you're prejudiced in our favor. Maybe you can explain things to the guys who've been grumbling. Tell that guy what I said about Cox. Coming from you, maybe he'll calm down."

Reese appeared thoughtful. "I'll do the best I can, of course."

"I know you will, Pee Wee."

Reese went quietly to work, as did Dodger vice-president Buzzy Bavasi when he found out about what was happening. It was a matter of straightening out the resentful thinking of five Dodger players, none of whom was deeply anti-Negro.

Several days later, Robinson was suiting up for an exhibition game at Miami when he was approached by the veteran Dodger pitcher whose misdirected sympathy for his friend Billy Cox started the racial antagonism.

"I just wanted to tell you one thing," the player said quietly. "For five years I've broken my back for you, and for five years you've broken your back for me. I'll still do it. No matter what you heard or what you think about anything else, that's all I want you to remember."

Robinson looked up at the man. "That's all I should remember and all I want to remember. It's the only way it should be."

The pitcher turned and walked back to his locker. It was all over . . .

It had stopped snowing. Jackie yawned and stretched. Once they'd gotten straightened away, what a team the Dodgers fielded that year! A real powerhouse, Jackie recalled. Clinched the pennant in the second week of September. He'd batted .329, played all over the place—left field, third base, second, first. Even one game at shortstop. Suddenly Jackie frowned. The memory of his itinerant fielding brought him back to reality.

For a long moment he gazed at his reflection in the big window. There was no escaping it. His hair was turning gray. He got up out of the chair. "I think I'm going to bed, Rae," he said to his wife.

She looked up at him, surprised. "At ten o'clock?"

Jackie shrugged. "All of a sudden I feel tired."

CHAPTER TWENTY

You prolong the inevitable when you're an athlete for money. You try to do with the experience of your years what your body did for you instinctively when you had it all. One day the ground ball gets by you that once you would have had in your hip pocket. The little looping fly ball drops in front of you for a hit. The change-up bothers you and the kid with the fast ball is blowing them right past your bat.

So you play position. You figure the batters more. You move in close on the banjo hitters and hope they don't bang one over your head because you'll never catch up with it. You move deep on the muscle boys and hope that kid shortstop can get back for the Texas leaguers.

You switch to a lighter bat. Then you try choking up on that one. You swing on the 3–1 pitch more. You learn to hit to the opposite field.

You have the good days, too. You wake up in

the morning and there's no pain. They can't hit a ball past you and you rap the fast ball out of the park.

That's when you know for sure—when you have the good days. Because it used to be that all the days were the good days, and you could only tell the difference when you had a bad one.

The miseries came to Jackie Robinson in 1954. In spring training he injured his knee and was side-lined for a week. Getting into shape used to be tough enough. Now it was agony. In a depressed mood one day in Florida, Jackie told the sports writers he hoped this would be his last year in baseball. If he'd gained the financial security he was seeking for his family by the end of the sea-son, he would call it a career.

The Dodgers made him their left fielder. It was a little easier there. In the infield he had to run a lot, start and stop quickly. His legs couldn't take that daily punishment any more.

Although Jackie was no Tris Speaker in the out-field, he was certainly adequate, and despite chron-ic knee conditions and a persistent heel injury, he led the Dodger offense through most of the 1954 season.

Robinson wasn't the only Dodger player be-low par physically. Catcher Roy Campanella was plagued with a bad hand that prevented him from gripping the bat firmly all season long. One of the greatest defensive catchers in the game, Roy was too valuable behind the plate to bench even though he was practically useless as a hitter.

With Campanella's powerful bat silent, the Dodgers' chances for a third straight pennant diminished considerably. Then pitcher Johnny Podres, the effective left-hander, dropped out with an appendicitis attack. Captain Reese came up with a leg injury. Half the pitching staff, at one time or another during the season, missed regular rotation because of a sore arm.

Robinson, battling to hold the Dodgers together, missed thirty games because of his leg conditions. With his stiff knees, sore heel and Charley horse, he nevertheless patrolled left field better than most healthy left fielders in the league. At the plate, he was still deadly in the clutch. But as soon as he started running down the first base line it was apparent this was not the same old Jackie.

He couldn't break away from the plate as quickly as he used to. They were getting him now on the slow hoppers he used to beat out. He didn't bunt as much for the base hit now, nor did he stretch singles into doubles, zip from first to third on a sacrifice.

It turned out to be the wrong season for Walter Alston to debut as Dodger manager. The humorless joke about Alston in 1954 was that the Dodger management had hired him to beat the Yankees in the

World Series—and he couldn't even win the pennant.

The Dodgers hung onto the Giants' tail grimly, but the Brooklyn club had too much going against it. Of the pitchers, only Carl Erskine was able to win consistently. Robinson, Reese and Snider carried the burden of the hitting attack, Jackie winding up with a .311 average.

But if some of the fire had gone from Robinson's flashing feet, it hadn't gone from his tongue. On June 2nd in Milwaukee, Jackie was thrown out of the game by umpire Lee Ballanfant, and subsequently fined fifty dollars by the league president. In September he was fined seventy-five dollars for what league president Giles said was ". . . conduct on the bench and remarks from your dressing room."

This was the aftermath of an argument in the ninth inning of a close game in September, when umpire Augie Donatelli called Pee Wee Reese out at first base. Reese was thrown out by Donatelli, which started Robinson going. In the dugout, Jackie stood up and wrapped a towel around his neck, a recognized baseball player's symbol for "choking up."

He kept a running verbal attack going against Donatelli for the remainder of the inning, and later in the Dodger shower room Jackie called out some uncomplimentary remarks about the umpire, knowing that the umpires' shower room was adjacent to that of the Dodgers'.

Robinson yelled even louder when he was hit with the fine. He complained that Giles was singling him out for punishment.

"That's something new, getting fined for something you say in your own clubhouse," Jackie stormed. "That's the fourth time Giles has fined me."

And for the umpteenth time, Jackie's wife Rae extracted a promise from him that he'd try to keep out of arguments.

"By now I should know it's useless to ask you, Jackie," she said to him, "but can't you let some other player argue with the umpires for once?"

Jackie grinned at her. "I promise. No more arguing with umpires."

When he headed for the Dodgers' training camp the following spring, Jackie repeated his promise. But he could no more keep out of arguments than he could keep from getting base hits. Having his say in a controversy on the field was as important to him as a stolen base. But he did keep half his promise for a while. Jackie's first big blowoff had nothing to do with an umpire; it was with manager Alston.

Jackie had watched his diet during the winter, and reported to Vero Beach in vastly improved shape. Moreover, his legs felt fine. The pains in his knees and heel seemed to be gone. He felt frisky and ready for a good year, he told reporters.

But as the spring exhibition swing got under way, Robinson found himself sitting on the bench more often than playing. It made him restless. He feared that the inactivity would throw him out of condition. And he made his usual mistake of revealing his irritation to one of the sports writers.

As a matter of course, Alston was asked to comment on Jackie's complaint. "If Robinson has any complaints let him come to me with them, not to the press," Alston said hotly.

Jackie came to his manager, and the two men engaged in a blistering verbal bout in the Dodgers' clubhouse that fairly shook the plaster off the walls. But when it was all over, the air was cleared and Jackie thought a lot more of Alston for taking him on.

The year before, he'd had occasion to brand his manager a "wooden Indian" for failing to back him up during an argument with an umpire.

The Dodgers were supremely confident they'd win the pennant in 1955, and they proved they were no dreamy optimists when they reeled off ten straight wins from opening day before being stopped.

Then the Giants came to Ebbets Field and Robinson was in the middle of another rhubarb; still not with an umpire, however. Sal Maglie, the perennial Dodger nemesis, the artist with the "brush-back" pitch, was on the mound for New York.

Maglie's usually fine control seemed to be off that day, particularly his control of the "brush-back." In the second inning, Sal threw two quick strikes to Robinson, then the next pitch came sailing right at Jackie's head. Robinson struck out on the next serve. He was so blinded with rage he missed the ball by a foot.

In the fifth inning, Jackie came up for the second time. On Maglie's first pitch he squared away to bunt, but let the pitch go by for ball one. However, Sal got Robinson's message. He remembered several years back, when he'd come close to Jackie with a couple of pitches, Robinson had bunted down the first base line and charged into him when he'd gone over to field the ball.

This was—and is—considered by many baseball men a sound anti-"duster" tactic.

Maglie remembered—and he wasn't having any today, thank you. On the next pitch, sure enough, Robinson bunted along the first base line, forcing first baseman Whitey Lockman off the bag to field the ball and—or so he thought—Maglie to first base to receive the throw.

Sal remained on the mound however, and second baseman Davey Williams raced over to cover first. Robinson, charging down the line, saw the uniform at first base, hardly noticing who the player was.

It was too late, however, to halt his charge when at the last split second he recognized Williams. Jackie hit the second baseman a solid blow with his left shoulder, sending him sprawling to the ground.

Maglie ran over to Williams. Shortstop Al Dark ran over to Robinson. Umpire Tom Gorman ran over to Dark. Then the players from both dugouts rushed out and ran over to everybody. No punches were thrown, but plenty of insults were hurled back and forth before the umpires cleared the field and play was resumed.

It was a brief truce. With two out in the Giants' half of the fifth, Dark hit a line drive into the left field corner. It was an easy double. But Dark preferred to try for a difficult triple, especially since Robinson was playing third base.

Jackie waited for the throw from left fielder Amoros, never dreaming that Dark would be trying for three bases. When he saw Dark charge around second base and head for third without hesitating, he had just enough time to say "Oh! Oh!" to himself. Then the throw came in from left field, in plenty of time to get Dark. But Alvin, a former football All-American himself, threw a rolling block at former All-American Robinson.

Dark, Robinson and the ball flew off in separate directions. Dark scrambled to his feet—safe with his triple. Robinson moved back to his position, hurling invectives at the Giants' shortstop. Dark came right back at him, and the two traded words until umpire Babe Pinelli stepped between them and ordered them to stop.

In the clubhouse after the game, which the Dodgers won, 3–1, Robinson was congratulated by the Brooklyn players for his bunt and charge at Williams. After the play, Maglie hadn't thrown close to a Dodger batter for the rest of the game.

Manager Alston walked over to Jackie and extended his hand. "Shake, Jackie. That was nice going."

Coach Billy Herman came over. "Jackie, give me your hand," he said. "You showed me something today. The ball quit slipping out of Maglie's hand after you hit Williams."

"I wasn't trying to hit Williams," Jackie began. "I thought—"

But every time he tried to tell his story another Dodger was stopping by to tell him what a great play it had been.

"Robinson," Pee Wee said to him, with mock seriousness, "you're always getting into trouble. I never saw a man for getting into trouble as much as you do."

The Dodgers continued to breeze through the league. But Robinson, after his quick start, fell off rapidly. His knees began to bother him again. In May he asked Alston to bench him for a few days. His average had dwindled to .244.

Jackie couldn't shake his slump. He couldn't figure what was wrong. The year before his knees had bothered him, yet he'd hit .311.

"You'll come out of it," Reese assured him. "You've been in slumps before."

By June it was no longer a slump. It appeared that Jackie had lost something at the plate. He compensated the best way he knew how. Forcing his aging legs to follow the commands of his mind, he became more daring on the bases. He tried to bunt more, to take the extra base, to force fielders into mistakes by bluffing and running.

"I've got to be doing things now," Jackie admitted to a sports writer. "I've got to keep moving and making the most of everything. It's the only way I can hang in there for as many games as I feel I should play. It's the only way I can be a real help to the club. If I can't do it one way, I've got to do it another."

He was still able to provide the excitement, the psychological lift. The feeling persisted with the Dodgers that they could pull any losing game out of the fire if Jackie was in the line-up.

"If a game lasts long enough, Robinson will find a way to beat you," a rival manager said of him.

His aggressive spirit was often an inspiration to the team. Not all of the Dodgers liked him personally, but all respected him as a great ballplayer. Even a couple of the more passive Negroes on the club never became very friendly with Jackie. His race consciousness made them uncomfortable.

But on the field it was different. To Don Newcombe, the big right-handed pitcher, Jackie was a constant needle, but a necessary one. When Newk pitched, Robinson kept a constant stream of chatter going at him, often deliberately abusive, calculated to needle Newcombe into bearing down.

In July Jackie injured his knee again, and he had to be helped off the field. After several days on the sidelines, a rumor circulated around the press box at Ebbets Field that this latest injury would mean the end of Robinson's playing career.

Reached at his home in Stamford, Jackie denied the report.

"I was told by Doc Wendler that it was a twisted knee, that's all. It may pop out from time to time, but I don't think that would have to end my career. At least I hope not."

"You said at the beginning of the season this might be your last year anyway," a reporter commented. "Does that still go?"

"That would depend," Jackie replied. "I'd like to play again next year. That would make me a ten-year man, you know, and I'd certainly like to earn those pension benefits for my family. On the other hand, I wouldn't want to stay on if I had to take a big cut in salary, and right now I'm not sure the Dodgers will be willing to pay my full salary next year.

"It wouldn't be worth while for me to stay on with a big cut. I'm all set with a contract now for a job outside of baseball, which calls for what I'm making now with the Dodgers."

"Who's the contract with?" he was asked.

"I can't reveal that now," Jackie said. "But it's to take effect on the first of January after I end my last season in baseball."

Though Jackie got back into the Brooklyn line-up shortly afterward, the knee continued to hobble him. He limped continually and was in and out of the line-up constantly. He played in only one hundred and five games that year and batted .256, both figures the lowest marks of his career.

Early in September the Dodgers clinched the pennant, then watched the windup of the American League race.

"I sure hope the Yankees win it," Robinson said. "It's my one ambition to beat those guys in the series before I leave baseball. And how many more chances will I get?"

As it turned out, one more chance was all Jackie and the Dodgers would need.

CHAPTER TWENTY-ONE

At first it appeared that the dismal pattern of recent years was to be repeated. The Dodgers had won five pennants since 1941. Five times they met the Yankees in the World Series, five times they were defeated. Now in the eighth inning of the first game in 1955 they were trailing 6–3, and it seemed to Jackie Robinson that in the Dodger dugout there was an air of resignation.

There's no spark, he thought grimly. We're playing like it's just another ball game. Some of the guys think the Yankees got us jinxed. We've got to do something to get a little spirit around here or we're dead ducks again. And this may be my last series . . .

"Let's go, Carl!" he called suddenly to Furillo, lead-off hitter in the eighth. "Let's start something here!"

Furillo responded with a single to center. Gil Hodges stepped in and Jackie moved up to the on-deck circle. "Get a hold of one, Gilly!" Robinson urged the Dodgers' big first baseman. But Hodges flied out to center field.

Jackie dug in and cocked his bat menacingly. He took a ball and a strike, then slammed a hot grounder that Gil McDougald couldn't hold. The ball spun away from the Yankee infielder and trickled into left field along the line. Jackie, running all the way, sped into second and Furillo went to third.

Don Zimmer flied out. Furillo and Robinson tagged up, Furillo scoring and Jackie going to third. It was a 6–4 game now. Frank Kellert came up to pinch-hit for Dodger relief pitcher Don Bessent.

Jackie took his lead off third base, watching Yankee hurler Whitey Ford. He recalled his own thoughts of a few moments before. We need some life. A spark. Something to give us a lift.

He widened his lead. Ford looked over at him. From the Yankee dugout a voice called to the hurler, "Don't worry about Robinson, Whitey. He ain't goin' nowhere!" Ford went into his windup—and Jackie took off for the plate. The startled pitcher hurried his throw. Yogi Berra grabbed it, but Jackie slid in ahead of the tag safely. It was the first time he'd stolen home in a World Series.

The Dodger players clapped Jackie on the back as he trotted into the dugout. "Nice work, Jackie!"

"That'll shake 'em up, Jack!" That was all the scoring for the Dodgers, however. They dropped the opener, 6–5. But at least Jackie had given them something to crow about.

When Tommy Byrne set Brooklyn back in the second game on five hits, 4–2, even Robinson felt a touch of hopelessness. In the Dodger clubhouse before the third game, the players held a brief meeting with Manager Walt Alston. When it was over, Jackie said to his teammates, "I don't know about you guys, but I'm getting sick and tired of the Yankees calling us a bunch of choke-ups. What do you say we go out today and knock 'em loose a little."

The Dodgers jumped on fireballer Bob Turley for two runs in the first inning. With two out and Reese on first, Campanella grabbed one of Turley's fast ones and rocketed it into the left field seats for a 2–0 bulge. The Yankees came back with two runs off Johnny Podres in the second to tie the score.

If the Dodgers were gong to fold, this was the excuse to do it, for the first two games of the series had opened the same way—the Dodgers getting a two-run lead, the Yankees tying the score, then winning the game. The Yankees appeared to have charmed lives in World Series competition, all right.

But not this time. Robinson wouldn't let his team

fold. With one out in the Dodger half of the second, Jackie singled to center. Amoros was hit in the back by a pitch, and pitcher Podres dropped a perfect bunt down the third base line to load the bases.

Turley stood on the mound, nervously juggling the ball. Jackie looked at him carefully. The young fireballer was upset, he could see that. And he was an erratic pitcher anyway. Jackie took a big lead off third and began to dance back and forth along the base line, trying to upset Turley further.

With only one out and the top of the Dodger batting order coming up, Robinson had no intention of trying to steal home. But he knew that Turley couldn't be sure of that. As the Yankee pitcher wound up to throw, Jackie ran halfway down the line and began shouting across to Amoros at second base.

"Watch me, Sandy. Watch me! When I go, you go, too, understand!"

Jackie's machinations had the desired effect on Turley. He pitched to Gilliam with one eye on third. Every time Turley wound up, Robinson churned down the line as far as he dared, then put on the brakes.

Gilliam walked on four pitches that missed the plate by a foot each time. Grinning widely, Jackie walked home with the tie-breaking run. Turley stomped around the mound, ready to blow sky high. Manager Casey Stengel took him out and replaced him with Tom Morgan, who promptly walked Reese to force in another run.

Jackie wasn't through with his base-running antics. In the seventh inning he lined a double down the left field line, or at least what would normally have been a double. As he rounded second he noticed that left fielder Elston Howard had come up with the ball and was facing toward second for the throw.

Robinson took his turn around the bag and a few extra steps, slowing as he did so, keeping his eyes on Howard, tempting the outfielder into throwing back of him in a pick-off attempt. The bluff worked. As Howard came down with his arm for the throw to second, Jackie, who had never come to a complete stop, turned the steam back on and made it to third standing up.

The maneuver was good for a run, too. With Robinson on third, the Yankee infield moved up close for a possible play at the plate. Amoros scored Jackie then with a bouncer through the right side that would have been an out had the Yankee infield been at its normal depth. The final score was 8–3, Brooklyn.

Jackie's base running had helped light the fire under the Dodgers. That kind of successful daring is infectious, and what's more, Jackie showed that the Yankees could get rattled under pressure, too.

So when the Yankees in the fourth game took a quick 3–1 lead, the Dodger hitters fairly itched to get up to the plate and get the runs back. In the fourth inning Campanella homered, Furillo singled and Hodges homered. Suddenly the score was 4–3 Brooklyn. The next inning Gilliam walked, Reese singled and Snider homered to break the game wide open. Final score, 8–5, and the series was tied at two games apiece.

The Dodgers were a hot ball club now. They took the Yankees three straight—5–3, in the fifth game, making a bit of history in the process. No team before in World Series competition had lost the first two games and come back to win the next three.

The battle reverted to Yankee Stadium for the sixth game. The rampaging Dodgers were out to make it an unprecedented four straight comeback, but the Old Pro Yankees didn't panic. Whitey Ford evened the series at three games apiece with a masterful four-hit, 5–1 victory.

In the Dodger clubhouse before the dramatic seventh game, Manager Alston was going over the Yankee hitters with Campanella and young Johnny Podres, winner of the third game of the series. Podres sat on a rubbing table, his feet hanging over the edge.

"Don't worry about a thing, skip," he said to

Alston. "These guys can't beat me. They're afraid of me."

Robinson, sitting near by, heard Podres' remark. He grinned. That was the kind of spirit he liked. He was burning with frustration himself at the moment, because he would have to miss this climactic game. His foot, which had begun to bother him in the fifth game, was beyond playing on at all now, and Don Hoak was taking his place at third base.

He got up then and hobbled over to Podres. "Listen, Johnny," he said, "you youngsters have plenty of time ahead of you. But this may be the last series for an old grayhead like me. And I'm busting to own one of those World Champion rings. Now how about getting one for me?"

The young hurler chuckled softly. "Robbie," he said, "you as good as got one."

It wasn't quite that easy. For three innings Podres and Tommy Byrne maintained a scoreless tie. Then with one down in the fourth, Campanella doubled, made it to third on an infield out and scored on a single by Hodges. It was 1–0, Brooklyn.

In the Yankee half of the inning, Podres induced Berra to lift a soft fly to center field. It was a routine chance, but Snider and Gilliam played Alphonse-Gaston with it till it dropped between them for a double.

Podres scuffed angrily at the dirt. Reese trotted over from short. "Easy, Johnny boy. Just take your time. Berra's staying right where he is."

Podres went back to work. He retired Hank Bauer on a fly to Furillo, Bill Skowron on a grounder to Don Zimmer at second and Bob Cerv on a pop fly to Reese.

The Dodgers got their pitcher another run in the fifth. Reese singled. Snider got a lift on an error. Campanella sacrificed both runners along. Furillo was intentionally passed, but Hodges stroked a long fly ball to center that scored Reese with the second run of the game. Hoak walked, reloading the bases.

George Shuba pinch-hit for Zimmer and grounded out. But the way things happened later in the game, the pinch-hitting strategy, successful or not, probably saved the day for Brooklyn. For with Zimmer out, Gilliam was shifted from left field to second base, with fleet-footed Sandy Amoros taking over the left field defense.

In the Yankees' sixth Martin led off with a walk. McDougald dropped a perfect bunt for a hit and the tying runs were on with nobody out. The dangerous Yogi Berra strode up to the plate. Campanella asked for time and trotted out to the mound.

"Let's keep it outside on this guy," he said to

Podres. "If he gets to pull one he'll hit it out of here sure."

Podres got Yogi to hit the outside pitch, but Yogi sliced it down the left field line. With Amoros swung around toward center field on the batter, hitting left-handed, the drive looked like a sure extra base hit.

But the game little Cuban never gave up on the ball. He flew like a startled deer across the outfield grass, while the crowd roared and the Dodgers silently urged Sandy on. As the ball started to fade and drop, Amoros lunged, stuck out his glove —and made the catch!

His momentum carried Sandy almost to the stands. He slid to a stop, wheeled and fired in the same motion toward shortstop. The throw was a little high. As Reese went into the air for the ball, he saw that McDougald had a long lead off first. Pee Wee came down with the ball, turned and whistled a bullet throw to Hodges, doubling off McDougald.

It was a picture play all around, a beautiful exhibition of defensive baseball at its best. And it stemmed the tide of the Yankee attack.

The Bronx Bombers made a last ditch bid in the eighth inning. Rizzuto singled. With one out, McDougald singled off Hoak's shoulder, sending Rizzuto to third. Again, with the tying runs on base, the dangerous Yogi Berra was up.

Reese walked to the mound. "You've got his number, Johnny. Remember, if he hits it back to you, come to me with it. Let's try to get two."

Podres nodded absently. He was looking at Berra. "One'll get you five Berra's gonna try to lose one."

The Dodger captain had to grin at the cool youngster. "He loses it and I'll lose you," he said. Then he trotted back to shortstop.

Podres went to work on Yogi. He got behind, two and one, then came in with a slow curve. Berra reached for the pitch, hit a short fly ball to Furillo for the second out. Then Podres fanned Hank Bauer.

The Dodger left-hander made a quick job of the Yankees in the ninth. Moose Skowron popped up. Bob Cerv struck out. Elston Howard grounded to Reese. Pee Wee threw across the diamond to Hodges—and the Dodgers were World Champions!

Dodger fans at Yankee Stadium went wild. They leaped out of the stands and broke through the cordon of special police to mob the Dodger players and Johnny Podres in particular. Then they ran into the street and stood outside the windows of the Dodger locker room and cheered their heroes until the clog of traffic forced the police to break up the demonstration.

In the borough of Brooklyn, it was New Year's Eve and the end of the war rolled into one madhouse celebration. The Dodgers were World Champions! All afternoon and night auto caravans roamed the streets of Brooklyn honking horns and tooting whistles. Kids marched through the streets banging on pots and pans. Some business offices closed down shop for the day. There were hot dogs on the house in neighborhood delicatessens. The Dodgers were World Champions! It was something no other Dodger team in history had been able to accomplish.

At the Dodgers' victory dinner Johnny Podres sought out Jackie Robinson. "Okay, old grayhead," he laughed to Jackie. "Now you can get into your slippers and retire to your scrapbooks. I got you that World Championship ring like I promised, didn't I?"

Jackie grinned at him. "Can't quit yet. Rae made me promise I'd give her the ring if we won. Now I'll have to come back next year and get one for myself."

CHAPTER TWENTY-TWO

IT is impossible to evaluate Jackie Robinson in the colorless language of statistics, though he is far from demeaned by the record books. But there is no way to assign a numerical equivalent to a rival pitcher's feelings about Jackie: "Given a particular situation where the next batter you face is the key man to either winning or losing a ball game, the one man in the National League I'd hate to see walk up to the plate, more than anyone else, is Jackie Robinson."

And under what classification can you put a veteran manager's opinion in a converse situation— "In one spot, in one ball game, where I need that one big base hit, I'd rather have Jackie Robinson up there for me than any man in the major leagues."

The emotional impact of Robinson on his own teammates and on rival players does not come through on a page of printed figures. As was quoted earlier, "If a game lasts long enough, Robinson will find a way to beat you."

There is no way to tabulate the number of mistakes he forced rival players to commit with his daring base running, and often with just the mere threat of his presence on the base. A veteran National League hurler once admitted, "With nobody on base and two out, I'd rather Robinson hit a home run off me than a single. I give up a run but I get him out of the way. When he's on first he upsets the whole team.

"Everybody starts playing with one eye on Robinson, including me, and it can blow up into a big inning. My catcher is leery of calling for a curve or a change-up on the next batter, because that gives Jackie an extra jump on the ball if he's stealing. And I feel the same way. Then the infielders start getting restless because Jackie may be going at any time, or if there's a ground ball you don't know how many bases he'll be trying to take on you.

"The same with the outfielders. If a base hit comes their way, the first thing they think of is how far is Robbie gonna try to go? Well, you can get the picture of what's happening. Sure as shootin' somebody's gonna be throwing the ball away and you're gonna see Robinson running home with a big grin on his face, and there's a big inning in the making.

"Just standing still off first base, Robinson can

raise more fuss in a ball park than any ballplayer I ever heard of."

No, nowhere in the columns of figures will you find the real greatness of Jackie Robinson. Other men had a better average, though not very many. But what Robinson meant to the Dodgers must be viewed in the light of actions of such men as Barney Shotton, who managed the Dodgers and kept Robinson in the line-up when it was obvious that leg injuries made it agony for Jackie to run out a ground ball.

"A one-legged Robinson does this club more good than any healthy guy I could sub for him," Shotton said in the heat of a pennant race. "With Robbie in there the boys have the feeling they're never out of it, that they can come from behind to win any ball game."

Jackie was acknowledged as one of the most consistently dangerous players in baseball, and yet he had the capacity to outdo himself in a clutch situation, to rise to an occasion with a super-rallying of his great skills.

This was never more evident, perhaps, than in the 1955 World Series. Robinson had experienced the worst season of his career. But he was determined to end the spell of the Yankees over the Dodgers in World Series competition. Ignoring the injuries to his knees that had plagued him all through the regular season, Jackie put on a dazzling display of base running in the first three games that inspired his teammates to their first World Championship.

The statistics for the 1955 series show only that Jackie's batting average was a lowly .182.

But statistics are bloodless, and there was never a more flesh-and-blood ballplayer than Jackie Robinson. You may not have liked Jackie, even if you wore a Dodger uniform, but you couldn't ignore his vital presence on the playing field.

Statistics? Robinson hit only .275 playing one hundred and seventeen games in 1956, but many followers of baseball consider it his finest year. His deep pride whipped him into renewed fighting shape. A younger player on a hot hitting streak benched him. But the Dodgers began to flounder and slide away from the league leaders.

It was then that a sports writer asked one of the Dodger veterans, "Do you still think you can win the pennant?"

The player glanced significantly at the Dodger bench. "We can with Robbie in there," he said.

And Robinson came up off the bench at the Dodgers' darkest hour. And he practically lifted them on his back and carried them along with him to victory through one of the most thrilling pennant races in recent years.

It is probable that Robinson calculated from the beginning that 1956 would be his last season in baseball. He wanted to be a ten-year man, not only for the generous pension benefits it meant, but ten years was a good round number for a man to be measured by in comparative baseball history.

Jackie didn't want that tenth year if it meant spending most of it on the Dodger bench, however. So when the Dodgers obtained third baseman Randy Jackson from the Chicago Cubs during the winter, Robinson knew he had his work cut out for him. He liked nothing better than a challenge to his ability. He met this one head on.

"Physically fit I'm a better ballplayer than Jackson," he told Dick Young of the New York *Daily News*. "And that's no reflection on him. I know the Brooklyn ball club got Jackson with the idea of playing him at third. But Jackson will have to beat me out of the job first."

The former Cub third baseman was seven years younger than Robinson. And it wasn't easy for Jackie to get his thirty-seven-year-old body into perfect playing condition. But he had that push of the direct challenge behind him. As usual he rose to it —and won. The afternoon before the first game of the season, manager Walter Alston announced his opening line-up. Robinson would be playing third base.

"I'm not disappointed in Jackson," Alston said.

"But it looks as though when Robinson sets his mind to it, he can beat out anybody."

In actual practice, Alston rotated Robinson and Jackson; he wasn't so sure that Jackie could play every day and last the season. Besides, he wanted a good look at Jackson. When Randy started suddenly on a hot hitting streak, Alston put him in the clean-up spot and kept Jackie on the bench.

For two weeks Robinson sat there while Jackson paced the Dodgers. Nevertheless they were steadily slipping out of contention in the pennant race. Milwaukee and Cincinnati were in front of them—and pulling away. Then the Braves came into town and beat the Dodgers for the seventh straight time. Brooklyn was five games behind now. The Braves had them set up for the kill.

Manager Alston had to make a move to stop the Dodgers' slide. On the night of July 31st, in Jersey City, Alston put Robinson back in the line-up against the Braves. That was the turning point of the Dodger fortunes.

Gene Conley started for the Braves against Carl Erskine. In the second inning Milwaukee picked up a run to take the lead. In the Dodger half of the second, Carl Furillo was on first base with a single. There was one out. Robinson came up for the first time in two weeks.

Conley got ahead of Jackie, one ball and two strikes. Then he came in with a curve and Jackie

234

belted it into the left field stands for a two-run home run. It was 2–1, Brooklyn. But in the ninth inning Eddie Mathews homered off Erskine to tie the score.

Reese opened the Dodgers' ninth with a single and was sacrificed to second. Then relief hurler Dave Jolly walked Furillo intentionally to get at Robinson. Percentages again. Theoretically, it was the right move. Psychologically, it was the wrong way to rub Robinson.

Jackie let a couple of pitches go by, then slammed a long drive to right center field that Billy Bruton made a great try for but couldn't quite reach. Reese loped around from second with the winning run of the game. Robinson had driven in all three of the tallies.

The Dodgers came alive then. They took the next one from the Braves again on Robinson's leadership. Jackie scored the winning run after getting himself into position with flashy base running.

With the score tied, Jackie sliced a single to right field. As he took his turn around first base, he saw that Bobby Thomson had bobbled the ball for a moment. That moment was enough for Jackie. He kept right on going and slid into second ahead of the throw.

The next batter grounded to the second baseman. Had Jackie remained on first, the ground ball would have been converted to a sure double play. Instead, the second baseman threw to first for the one out, and Robinson went on to third. A moment later he scored the winning run of the game on a pinch-hit single by Dale Mitchell.

Brooklyn moved right back into the race. Robbie was in there now. The Dodgers soon were fighting in a grueling, exciting three-way pennant race along with Cincinnati and Milwaukee.

Pacing the Dodger pitching staff was a strange newcomer—Sal Maglie. The year before, the Giants had traded him to the Indians, considering their one-time ace and Dodger nemesis all washed up. The Indians decided the same thing, after giving Sal a few innings of relief work.

The Dodgers had a hunch, though, that their former bitter enemy had enough left to help them out. And baseball being what it is, the Dodger players welcomed him to the team. As it turned out, Maglie made one of the most spectacular comebacks in baseball history, including a no-hit game among thirteen key victories in the Dodger pennant chase.

Into the middle of September the Dodgers, Braves and Reds continued their battle, with usually no more than three games separating the leader from the third place team. On the sixteenth of September, the Dodgers beat the Reds, 3–2, and moved into the league lead.

Before the day's game, Cincinnati manager

Birdie Tebbetts was watching the Dodgers take their batting practice. In the cage at the moment was Robinson. Tebbetts nodded toward Jackie and said to a near-by sports writer, "At a time like this, if I were managing their team I'd rather have Robinson coming up to bat than any ballplayer in the whole country. If he walked up there on his knees he'd be more dangerous than anybody else."

Considering that the Reds were in the pennant fight themselves, it was probably scant consolation to Tebbetts that Robinson proved his words true so quickly. Jackie led off the second inning with a double that started a two-run rally.

But on September 26th the Dodgers were in second place again, half a game behind the Braves. That night the Dodgers took on the Phillies at Ebbets Field. The scoreboard showed that the Braves had won their afternoon game, to give them the half game margin. If the Dodgers lost this one, they'd be a full game behind with but four games left to play.

The thirty-nine-year-old Sal Maglie and the thirty-seven-year-old Jackie Robinson combined spectacularly to keep the Dodgers in the race.

Jackie opened the Dodger offensive in the second inning with a double. Amoros went out, but Hodges walked. With Furillo up at the plate, Jackie began to dance off second, bluffing a steal. Philadelphia pitcher Jack Meyer watched Jackie, then whirled and tried to pick him off. He threw wildly into center field. Jackie sped to third and Hodges to second.

Furillo hit the next pitch slowly down to shortstop. Robinson charged for the plate. Shortstop Roy Smalley grabbed the ball, but it was too late to get Jackie at home. He threw Furillo out at first —and the Dodgers led, 1–0.

It would have been enough, the way Maglie was going to pitch that night, but Campanella homered to make it 3–0. Two more runs in the third inning made it 5–0.

Maglie, meanwhile, was breezing through the Phillies, while the tension mounted in Ebbets Field. This was Maglie's biggest night. In the ninth inning not a person in Ebbets Field dared utter an unnecessary sound for fear of jinxing the Dodger pitcher. Then when Marv Blaylock bounced out to Gilliam at second to end the game, the stands rocked with noise. Sal Maglie, "The Barber," once the Dodgers' bitterest foe, had pitched a no-hitter!

The pennant race went down to the last day of the season. Cincinnati had been eliminated several days before, but now, on the final day, the Dodgers held a half-game lead again, and Milwaukee had finished its schedule the day before. The Dodgers were assured of at least a tie. But after this heartstopping battle to the wire, they were in no mood for a play-off.

Don Newcombe pitched one of his shakier games, but held on for an 8–6 pennant-clinching victory, Don's twenty-seventh win of the campaign.

Newcombe later was to be voted the National League's Most Valuable Player, and would receive the first Cy Young award as the major league's Most Valuable Pitcher. But he'd still fall victim to the World Series jinx the Yankees had cast on him.

And Jackie Robinson would have to do without his second World Champion ring.

The Yankees took the World Championship title back from the Dodgers in a history-making seven-game series. Yankee pitcher Don Larsen was the history-maker, hurling a perfect game no-hitter in the fifth contest, the first perfect game ever pitched in a World Series.

Robinson saved the Dodgers from going down in six games. It was really the Yankees' own fault. They walked a man intentionally to pitch to Robinson, and as so many hurlers experienced during Jackie's ten-year career, this effrontery to his hitting skill was answered with a game-winning blow.

It came about in the tenth inning of the sixth game. The Yankees had won three contests, the Dodgers two. Bob Turley of the Yankees was locked in a scoreless tie with Clem Labine of the Dodgers. With one out in the tenth, Turley walked Jim Gilliam. Reese sacrificed. Since the winning run was represented by Gilliam at second base, the percentage, of course, was to walk Duke Snider, thereby creating a possible double play situation.

Which is what the Yankees did. Turley walked Snider and pitched to Robinson. Jackie promptly blasted one of Turley's fast balls over the head of Enos Slaughter in left field for a 1–0 Dodger victory.

It was a poetically fitting finale for Jackie Robinson that his last base hit in baseball should come in the tenth inning to win the game that tied the World Series.

That's how it was. In the deciding game, Johnny Kucks blanked the Dodgers, 9–0, holding Jackie hitless. To complete the history, on his last at-bat Jackie struck out to end the ball game, the World Series—and the baseball career of Jackie Robinson.

Yogi Berra dropped the third strike and was forced to throw Jackie out at first base. It was better that way. At least Jackie went out of baseball running.

CHAPTER TWENTY-THREE

THE entry of Jackie Robinson into organized baseball was accompanied by a storm of controversy. His eleven years in baseball were filled with controversy. What, then, but that his retirement from baseball should be surrounded with controversy, too?

A confusion of chronology seems to have been the underlying cause of the series of acrimonious exchanges among Robinson, Dodger vice-president Buzzy Bavasi and several sports writers. In addition, there were accusations of quotes, misquotes, lies and double crosses. So much smoke and confusion surrounded the affair that the exact sequence of events probably will never be agreed upon.

It is definite that on December 10, 1957, the Dodgers made a deal to sell Jackie Robinson to the Giants for pitcher Dick Littlefield and thirty thousand dollars. Two days later, Chub Feeney of the Giants contacted Robinson, asking him if he intended to play with the Giants—or retire. If Jackie intended to retire, Feeney said, there would be no sense in making the announcement of the trade to the newspapers.

"I'll have to think about it," Jackie replied. "I'm at the point now where I don't know for certain what I'll do next year."

On the basis of Jackie's answer, Feeney released the story of the trade to the newspapers. It created a sensation. For ten years Robinson had been identified with the Brooklyn Dodgers. It hardly seemed possible to either Giant or Dodger fans that Jackie would now don the uniform of his once bitterest rivals.

The Giant players were ready to receive Robinson as cordially as the Dodger players had welcomed Sal Maglie the year before. After all, Robinson had been murdering them for years. It might be nice to have him playing for them, instead of against them.

Meanwhile, Jackie was hedging in his comments to the sports writers. He repeated his statement to Feeney that he wasn't quite sure of his plans for next year. At the same time, he did say, according to Jim McCully of the New York *Daily News,* "I'm going to do all I can for the Giants . . ."

For the next two weeks, it appeared that Robinson was trying to make up his mind either to accept a Giant contract, or retire from baseball.

The truth, however, was that he had decided weeks earlier that he was going to retire. When the Giants' Chub Feeney had first phoned him to talk about the trade, he had been preparing an article for *Look* Magazine, revealing his plan to retire from baseball and become vice-president of the Chock Full O' Nuts Company, a nationwide restaurant chain.

Jackie was unable to reveal his plan to Feeney, however, because his contract with *Look,* made two years earlier, gave them an exclusive story on his retirement plans. Naturally, the magazine wasn't ready to have the story released until the time the issue was distributed around the country.

On January 6th, the *Look* story broke. In it, Jackie said that he had decided to quit baseball. He realized he'd reached the end of the line. "I'm 38 years old with a family to support," Jackie said. "I've got to think of the future and about security.

"At my age, a man doesn't have much future in baseball and very little security . . . After you've reached your peak, there's no sentiment in baseball. You start slipping and pretty soon they're moving you around like a used car . . . I didn't want that."

Immediately, Jackie was criticized by some of the sports writers, and by Dodger executive Buzzy

Bavasi, for leading everyone to believe that he might play with the Giants, when he'd decided weeks before to retire.

"I didn't want to mislead anybody," Jackie said. "But two years ago I had contracted to give *Look* the exclusive story of my retirement, whenever it would happen. I couldn't reveal the contents of the story before *Look* was ready for me to, and at the same time, I tried to avoid a direct statement that I would play for the Giants."

As a matter of fact, up to that point there had actually been a slight chance that Jackie would reconsider his decision and play with the Giants. The Chock Full O' Nuts Company was willing to let Jackie play another year.

But the sharpness of some of the criticism leveled against him killed that slight chance. Angrily, Jackie told reporters, "One million dollars could not induce me to change my mind!"

There it remained, though until Robinson formally submitted his retirement request to the National League offices, there continued to be speculation that Jackie would play baseball in 1957.

Hardly had this controversy cooled off before Jackie was in the middle of another one. In a speech before a church group in Waukegan, Illinois, Jackie charged that one of the reasons the Milwaukee Braves lost the pennant was that several of the players had been doing too much night-clubbing during the final weeks of the season.

The Braves hotly denied it. Most of the sports writers had good reason to believe it was true, but Jackie was criticized nevertheless for "popping off" about it in public.

Jackie apologized. "I know I shouldn't have said it," he admitted. "But I never thought it would be printed. It was just a small church gathering. I had no idea there was even a reporter there, or I probably wouldn't have said it at all."

One of the biggest reasons for Jackie's propensity for getting involved in controversy was his honesty. "If somebody asks me a direct question, what else can I do but give them an honest answer?" Jackie used to say.

It was this forthright attitude of his that caused another rhubarb in short order. Jackie, discussing the Dodgers' pennant chances for 1957, was relating his opinions of Dodger ballplayers to Milton Gross, sports columnist for the New York *Post*. As usual, Jackie gave honest, but hardly diplomatic, answers to Gross's questions.

Robinson was asked about Roy Campanella. "I think he's about done," Gross quoted Jackie as saying. "I don't think he can come back off last season's record and have another great one like he did twice before. After a while so much of what you have goes. I hope not but I think it's gone with Roy."

It was to be expected that Campanella would challenge Jackie's statement. The Dodger catcher, a mild-mannered man, charged hotly that Jackie was "just shooting off his mouth."

The weeks attending Jackie's retirement announcement had their pleasanter moments, too. Interspersed among the warlike communiques in the newspapers were reports of additional honors for Robinson.

He was awarded the annual Spingarn Medal by the National Association for the Advancement of Colored People, and the annual sportsmanship award of the B'nai B'rith Sports Lodge in New York City. And several of the sports writers predicted in their columns that before long Jackie would be voted into baseball's Hall of Fame.

Later, after he had settled down in his new capacity as vice-president and personnel manager of the restaurant chain, Jackie received an honorable Doctor of Laws degree from Howard University. And in June, Governor Abraham Ribicoff of Connecticut appointed Jackie a member of the state's new parole board.

The talk lingered for a while longer that Jackie would be back in baseball someday. But there was to be no more baseball for him; not as a player, at least. He traded in his old No. 42 for a neat business suit. When his executive job allowed he took the time for a trip to Ebbets Field to see his former teammates play their last season there before moving to a new home in Los Angeles. It was as though his retirement had been the signal for an end to the entire saga of the Brooklyn Dodgers. In 1958 they would still be the Dodgers —but the Los Angeles Dodgers.

Did Jackie miss baseball? The question was asked of him often during the first year of his retirement, though many a sports writer commented that whatever Robinson's sentiments, baseball probably missed him more than he missed baseball.

No doubt he missed the excitement, the flavor, the thrills of competition. But he told one sports writer that summer of 1957 that he was perfectly content with his new life. "Rae and I can live together like a normal family now," he said. "I can spend more time with the children. There are so many things I have to catch up on, things I was forced to neglect when I was traveling with the Dodgers."

So while the Dodgers moved west after losing the 1957 race to the Braves, Jackie remained in New York with Chock Full O' Nuts. As the years flew past he added a little weight around the middle, a little gray to his hair, and a further, climactic laurel to an already honor-studded career.

As he was the first Negro to play in Organized

Baseball, so, in 1962, did he become the first Negro to be elected to baseball's Hall of Fame.

Two years later he left his job to work on the presidential nomination campaign of New York's Governor Rockefeller. Then, at last, Jackie returned to his first and greatest love—baseball. In 1965 he was hired by the National Broadcasting Company to work on its special Saturday baseball telecast, "Championship Baseball," as an announcer and commentator with sportscaster Chris Schenkel.

Jackie's return to the baseball scene, even in so limited an area, gave rise to new speculations about his further activities. Would he remain a sportscaster or try for a more active role? A coach perhaps?

There was one rumor in the summer of 1965 that caused more excitement than all the rest. With the venerable Casey Stengel due to retire as manager of the Mets at the end of the season—would Jackie Robinson become the first Negro manager?

The hapless but colorful Mets—indeed all of baseball, it was said, could use such a man.

LIFETIME RECORD: JOHN ROOSEVELT (JACK...

Born January 31, 1919, Cairo, Georgia ... ...ed right, threw right

Year	Club	League	Pos.	G.	AB.	R.	H.	2B.	3B.	HR.	RBI.	B.A.
1946—Montreal		Int.	2B	124	444	**113	155	25	8	3	66	*.349
1947—Brooklyn		Nat.	1B	151	590	125	175	31	5	12	48	.297
1948—Brooklyn		Nat.	2-1-3B	147	574	108	170	38	8	12	85	.296
1949—Brooklyn		Nat.	2B	156	593	122	203	38	12	16	124	.342
1950—Brooklyn		Nat.	2B	144	518	99	170	39	4	14	81	.328
1951—Brooklyn		Nat	2B	153	548	106	185	33	7	19	88	.338
1952—Brooklyn		Nat.	2B	149	510	104	157	17	3	19	75	.308
1953—Brooklyn		Nat.	INF-OF	136	484	109	159	34	7	12	95	.329
1954—Brooklyn		Nat.	OF-INF	124	386	62	120	22	4	15	59	.311
1955—Brooklyn		Nat.	INF-OF	105	317	51	81	6	2	8	36	.256
1956—Brooklyn		Nat.	INF-OF	117	357	61	98	15	2	10	42	.275

Major League Totals .... 1382 4877 947 1518 273 54 137 734 .311

†Traded to New York Giants for Pitcher Dick Littlefield and reported $35,000, December 13, 1956; Robinson announced retirement from game, January 5, 1957 cancelling trade.

WORLD SERIES RECORD

Year	Club	League	Pos.	G.	AB.	R.	H.	2B.	3B.	HR.	RBI.	B.A.
1947—Brooklyn		Nat.	1B	7	27	3	7	2	0	0	3	.259
1948—Brooklyn		Nat.	2B	5	16	2	3	1	0	0	2	.188
1952—Brooklyn		Nat.	2B	7	23	4	4	0	0	1	2	.174
1953—Brooklyn		Nat.	OF	6	25	3	8	2	0	0	2	.320
1955—Brooklyn		Nat.	3B	6	22	5	4	1	1	0	1	.182
1956—Brooklyn		Nat.	3B	7	24	5	6	1	0	1	2	.250

World Series Totals .... 36 137 22 32 7 1 2 12 .234

* Denotes led league.
** Denotes tied for league lead.

Voted Most Valuable Player, 1949.
Elected to Hall of Fame, 1962.